T0048306

The United States Constitution
and Citizens' Rights

The United States Constitution and Citizens' Rights

The Interpretation and Mis-Interpretation of the American Contract for Governance

by ROLAND ADICKES

McFarland & Company, Inc., Publishers
Jefferson, North Carolina, and London

Library of Congress Cataloguing-in-Publication Data

Adickes, Roland, 1930–
    The United States Constitution and citizens' rights : the
interpretation and mis-interpretation of the American
contract for governance / by Roland Adickes.
        p.   cm.
    Includes index.

    ISBN-13: 978-0-7864-0929-7
    softcover : #55 alkaline paper ∞

    1. Constitutional law—United States.   2. Constitutional
amendments—United States.   3. Constituent power—
United States.   I. Title.
KF4550.A723   2001
342.73'02—dc21   2001018058

British Library cataloguing data are available

©2001 Roland Adickes. All rights reserved

*No part of this book may be reproduced or transmitted in any form
or by any means, electronic or mechanical, including photocopying
or recording, or by any information storage and retrieval system,
without permission in writing from the publisher.*

Cover image ©2001 Photo Spin

Manufactured in the United States of America

*McFarland & Company, Inc., Publishers
    Box 611, Jefferson, North Carolina 28640
    www.mcfarlandpub.com*

To my grandson
Dean Andrew Adickes

so he may understand that, once upon a
time, long before he was born, this country
governed itself in accordance with a written
Constitution—and not by the mere
legal fictions of today.

"...I merely propose to make legislature and court alike responsible to the sober and deliberate judgment of the people, who are musters of both legislature and courts."

Theodore Roosevelt

Contents

Preface   1

On Sources   3

Introduction: What's the Problem?   7

I.   The Expansion of the Powers of Congress   21

II.   The Expansion of the Judicial Power   45

III.   Education   60

IV.   Housing   77

V.   Americans with Disabilities   84

VI.   Air   94

VII.   Water   101

VIII.   Endangered Species   110

IX.   The Arts   122

X.   Prisons   129

XI.   What Can and Should We Do?   150

Index   163

Preface

Among the books in my home is one called *Voices of the Civil War*. It is a compilation of quotations from letters, diaries and other writings of both Northern and Southern officers and soldiers fighting in the same battles. It does not read as smoothly as an historian's narrative might, but you get more of a feel for what people who were there experienced, felt and thought.

You will encounter something similar in parts of this book, "Voices of the Constitution" you might call it, in the form of passages from the writings of American statesmen, Supreme Court justices, judges, lawyers, commentators, and journalists who disputed, created, and applied the Constitution.

As I progressed with this book I came to stand more and more in awe of the intellectual effort of these outstanding people, through two centuries, and of the prescience of some of them as to what would happen if a given phrase in the Constitution were to be interpreted one way or another.

I could have picked a few phrases from the long quotations and told you the rest in a predigested narrative. But that would not serve my purpose. I believe we need to listen at length to these voices of the American past if we want to keep the heritage of self-government. Besides, I would rather have someone talk who has already been recognized as qualified for the task.

For my own qualifications, I claim some common sense and a legal education; the two are not always incompatible. I am a retired California government lawyer. I have used the work of scholars, notably my constitutional law teacher, the late Philip Kurland, but this book is not a book of scholarship. It is an attempt to read the Constitution as it is written, in plain English, together with the comments of outstanding Americans.

I propose to act as a tour guide, so to speak, through some parts of the Constitution. It is the business of tour guides to show people through ancient ruins and tell them how grand they were when they were new. The Constitution is a partial ruin. The walls are still standing, but the roof has collapsed in some spots and it leaks in other places. The complete shelter the Founders built against an overweening federal government is no more. It's raining through on some Americans. But the majority are still in the dry, are comfortable, probably are not even aware that it's raining through on some of their fellow citizens and that, if the roof isn't fixed, it will rain through on themselves. I hope to persuade you in this book to do something about fixing the roof.

I will now introduce myself, as tour guides do. I was born in Germany in 1930 and grew up there. So as a boy I was an enemy alien— without my informed consent, I should add. After the war I became a friendly alien, being a citizen of the Federal Republic of Germany, a country allied with the United States in the common defense effort.

In 1954 I hit the jackpot. I was given a one year Fulbright scholarship to the United States, to the University of Chicago, to be precise. I liked it so well in the United States that I came back as soon as I could, and stayed. In 1961, after I had received my law degree, I came out to California where I have lived ever since.

I should add an additional justification for writing this book. Twice in my life I have sworn to defend and uphold the Constitution: Once when I became a citizen; the second time when I became a lawyer.

By my lights, the Constitution needs defending right now. I hope I can convince you of that with this book.

On Sources

The first and foremost source is, of course, the Constitution of the United States. The original text contains only article and section numbers. It has become customary to assign numbers to the paragraphs or clauses within a section. I have followed this custom, so, for example, Article I, Section 8, Clause 1 refers to the first paragraph in Section 8.

For "contemporary" comments, my second source on the Constitution is the five volume work *The Founders' Constitution*, edited by Philip Kurland and Ralph Lerner (University of Chicago Press, 1987). This work is cited as Kurland, followed by the volume, page and item number, the year, and sometimes a short reference to the sources from which the editors drew the material, for example: "Kurland, Vol. 4, p. 305, No. 65, *Martin v. Hunter's Lessee* [1816])."

By "contemporary" I am referring to the people who participated in the public debate at the creation of the Constitution or in the continuing public controversy during the first several decades of the Republic, in the period from the late 1780s to the mid–1840s. The following time frame may be helpful:

- The Constitutional Convention met in 1787, in the twelfth year of American Independence.
- Benjamin Franklin died in 1790, about one year after the new government had been established.
- Thomas Jefferson and John Adams died in 1826.
- Chief Justice John Marshall died in 1835.
- James Madison died in 1836.
- Justice Joseph Story died in 1845.

The third source is the reported opinions of the United States Supreme Court. These are reported in the *United States Reports, Cases*

Adjudged in the Supreme Court... published by the U.S. Government Printing Office. During the first half of the 19th century the Court's opinions and counsels' arguments were collected and printed by private individuals, beginning with A.J. Dallas, who collected decisions of the courts of Pennsylvania and later included decisions of the U.S. Supreme Court, and William Cranch, who collected solely the decisions of the U.S. Supreme Court.

After the government took over the publication of the opinions of the Court, the earlier reports were incorporated into the *United States Reports*, so the volume number and the abbreviated name of the reporter appear together with the volume and page of the official reports, for example: *Marbury v. Madison* (1803) 5 U.S. (1 Cr.) 137. This translates into: Volume 5 of the *United States Reports* (Volume 1 of Cranch's reports) p. 137.

In addition to the official reports, there are two private editions of the opinions of the United States Supreme Court:

1. The *United States Supreme Court Reports, Lawyers' Edition*, published by Lexis Law Publishing, which is cited as L Ed or L Ed 2d (the "Second Series" was begun in 1956).

2. The *United States Supreme Court Reporter, Cases Argued and Determined in the Supreme Court of the United States* published by the West Publishing Company, cited as S Ct.

Thus a complete citation for an older case is: *Weems v. United States* (1910) 217 US 349, 54 L Ed 793, 30 S Ct 544; and for a more recent case: *Estelle v. Gamble* (1976) 429 US 97, 50 L Ed 2d 251, 97 S Ct 285.

The opinions of the federal Courts of Appeals are published by the West Publishing Company in the *Federal Reporter*, which is cited as F, and F2d and F3d for the second and third series, respectively, with the volume number preceding and the page number following, for example: *United States v. Ohio Department of Highway Safety* (1980) 635 F2d 1195.

The occasional opinions of the federal District Courts are also published by the West Publishing Company, in the *Federal Supplement*, cited as FS, again with volume number preceding and page number following.

The next source are Acts of Congress. These are found in the

United States Statutes at Large, published by the U.S. Government Printing Office, and cited as, for example, 39 Stat. 929, meaning volume 39,
page 929 of the *Statutes*. Most of the Acts of Congress are also found
in the *United States Code*. I have used the *United States Code Annotated*,
published by the West Publishing Company, which is cited as, for example, 42 USCA Section 12102. The number preceding the abbreviation
refers to the Title of the *Code*, not the volume. Most Titles contain several volumes.

You will probably be able to find these reports and statutes in your
county law library.

Introduction:
What's the Problem?

We, the citizens of the United States, are in danger of losing the power to govern ourselves in accordance with a written Constitution, our Constitution.

How can this be? Congress and the Supreme Court have, in effect, amended the Constitution, changing our form of government from the one described in the Constitution, in which the federal government is to take care of defense, foreign policy, commerce regulation and a few other matters (see Chapter I), to one in which the federal government legislates on nearly everything and mandates the states to carry out its laws.

We, the citizens, have not been able to have our say on these amendments. Many of these amendments we would no doubt ratify in whole or in part when made aware of them, but others we would not.

Here are some examples of these amendments:

1) The Court has extended federal power to the issue of abortion and to state prisons.
2) Congress has extended federal power to urban housing, education, disabled persons, the arts and the environment.

But isn't the Supreme Court the ultimate authority and doesn't the Court step in when Congress or the president go beyond their constitutional bounds? Not so. We, the citizens are ultimately responsible.

By its own doctrine the Court "steps in" only when a case or controversy is brought before it. The Court's decision, while precedent for future cases, is "law" only for the case it decided (see Chapter II).

We, the citizens are the ultimate authority on the Constitution. It is up to us to rein in any branch of the federal government which over-steps its constitutional bounds.

The Constitution is a written agreement to which all citizens are parties. You became a party when you were born a U.S. citizen or, if foreign born, when you swore allegiance to the Constitution. It is the law of the land, but it is not, with the exception of a few legal terms of art, a technical legal document that only lawyers can properly understand. (See for examples of technical terms: Article I, Section 8, Clause 1; Article II, Section 4; Article III, Section 3, Clause 2.) You have heard the old saw that war is too important to be left to the generals. Well, the Constitution is too important to be left, entirely, to the lawyers. The common sense of the citizens must ultimately determine what it means.

The Constitution may be a bit hard to understand in some parts because most of it was written more than 200 years ago. But it is a living agreement, in force right now. So how do we read it? Limited to the meaning of 200 years ago, or with today's meaning? We have no real choice. We must read it with today's meaning because despite all the scholarship which has been devoted to this, we cannot know one hundred percent what the Framers meant when they used certain words or phrases. Moreover, the Framers were not of one mind. The Constitution was a political compromise, as, for example, the provisions regarding slavery make glaringly clear. So we can use for guidance the pronouncements of the Framers, the pronouncements of the Supreme Court, and our historical practice, but ultimately it is up to the majority of the citizens to determine what the Constitution means, in today's plain English, for us.

At least some of the Framers agreed that this is the way to read the Constitution: "In relation to [a non-technical] subject, the natural and obvious sense of its provisions ... is the true criterion of construction" (*The Founders' Constitution*, edited by Philip Kurland and Ralph Lerner, Chicago and London: University of Chicago Press, 1987, Vol. 4, p. 401, No. 17, Hamilton, *The Federalist*, No. 83 [1788]. *The Founders' Constitution* will be referred to as Kurland). "The words are to be taken in their natural and obvious sense, and not in a sense unreasonably restricted or enlarged" (Kurland, Vol. 4, p.305, No. 65, *Martin v. Hunter's Lessee* [1816]).

But, while the meaning of some constitutional words may have been obscured over time, the words which are the heart of the matter are understandable enough to show you where Congress and the Court have gone outside the agreement.

Clearly the federal government created by the Constitution was a government limited to enumerated powers. There is a list of matters on which Congress may legislate (Article I, Section 8). There is also an express statement that anything not on that list is reserved to the states or the people (Tenth Amendment).

The matters on the list all have to do with what each state separately could not handle: common defense, that is, defense of all Americans and of all states in the Union together; a postal system operating throughout all the states; regulation of commerce with foreign nations; regulation of commerce from state to state; a common currency for all the states, rather than each state having its own money. And so on (see Chapter I).

This arrangement specifically leaves the power to legislate about all other matters to the states (Tenth Amendment), subject to the limits the people in each state have put into their state constitutions and subject to a list of matters prohibited to the states by the federal Constitution (Article I, Section 10).

In contrast, most state constitutions list only the matters which their legislatures are prohibited from touching, but otherwise leave them free to legislate about any subject matter their members consider appropriate.

So Congress and the state legislatures were intended to work under quite different ground rules. The state legislatures can do anything that's not expressly forbidden. *Congress can do only what is expressly permitted*, only what is found on the list in the Constitution.

For any law it enacts, Congress must be able to point to a word or phrase in the Constitution which authorizes Congress to legislate on that subject. Now read the Constitution and ask yourself where it authorizes federal legislation on education, public housing, disabled persons, the fine arts, abortion, speed limits, endangered species, clean air, wetlands, and so forth.

I think you will find that none of these are mentioned in the Constitution. So how come Congress has for years legislated on these subjects? Well, the lawyers will tell you that all of these subjects are "implied" in some other words or phrases of the Constitution.

Which words or phrases? Here's one of the clauses to which the lawyers will point you:

9

> The Congress shall have Power To lay and collect Taxes ... to pay the Debts and provide for the common Defence and general Welfare of the United States; ... [Article I, Section 8, Clause 1].

Start with the phrase "general Welfare." Cannot education, public housing, speed limits and so forth all be described as being part of the "general Welfare?" Arguably they can, but then are not all matters specifically mentioned in the Constitution *also* part of the "general Welfare?" Are not a common currency, post offices, patents, copyrights, uniform bankruptcy laws, standards of weights and measures, and, for that matter, an army and a navy to protect us and our commerce—all a part of "general Welfare"?

So why didn't the Founding Fathers just write: Congress shall have power to legislate for the general welfare of the United States, period? Why did they make the detailed list which would be quite unnecessary if they had meant to give Congress the general power to legislate on anything Congress deems appropriate—and supersede the states in everything?

When the lawyers tell you that a power to legislate about education, public housing, and everything else that Congress can think of is "implied" in some phrase such as "general Welfare," taken out of its context in the Constitution, they really directly contradict the plan of the Framers to create a federal government of enumerated powers and not a government that would legislate about everything and supersede the states.

On this point we have some guidance from the Framers. When the Constitution was presented for ratification in 1787, one of the arguments raised against the power to lay and collect taxes to provide for the common defense and general welfare of the United States was that it allegedly amounted to "an unlimited commission to exercise every power which may be alleged to be necessary for the common defense or general welfare" (*The Federalist*, No. 41).

The authors of *The Federalist* (who were among the most fervent supporters of a strong federal government) countered this argument by pointing out that the clause stating this power in a general way *was limited by the enumeration of the particular powers* following it (Article I, Section 8). They stressed repeatedly the point that Congress, as distinguished from the state legislatures, does not have "the whole power of legislation" (*The Federalist*, No. 32, 33, 41, 55, 83).

Interpreting the Constitution in a way that directly contradicts the Framers makes no sense. But how can we agree on the meaning of the old words? One way is to look at the substance of what they describe and translate it into current terms. For example, the Constitution authorizes Congress to create an army and a navy. In 1789 there was no other way of defending the nation than by wooden sailing ships with bronze cannon, and bodies of infantry, cavalry and artillery with the sabres and firearms then available. The substance of the words "army" and "navy" thus can reasonably be described as defense with the latest means of technology. So we can accommodate an air force, missiles, and lasers without distorting the meaning of the Constitution. Similarly, the power given to establish a post office and post roads—then the latest means of transmitting information nationwide—may be reasonably read to give Congress the power to provide for nationwide transmission of information by the latest technology. Of course, having that power does not mean that Congress must use it. Today the private sector is giving us nationwide information by the most current means.

The Framers knew that things would change and therefore provided for amending the Constitution. So why not amend by striking out "army" and "navy" and putting in new words to read: "defense forces based on any means available to defend the United States on the planet Earth, in the solar system, and in outer space." Why not? Because it would be a waste of time. Very few citizens will deny that the words "army" and "navy" must mean any and all possible means of defense. So we can save amendments for where they are necessary. For example, when a new power is to be given to the federal government, like Prohibition, or when an existing power is to be taken away, also like Prohibition; or when a power not mentioned in the Constitution but exercised by Congress is to be ratified, with proper conditions, like the power to regulate the environment—all examples of amendments that would be necessary.

The power to regulate the environment, like the power to levy the income tax, is one for which the Framers made no provision in the original Constitution. And, unlike the case of the income tax, there has been no amendment giving Congress the new power to regulate the environment. So how come Congress has legislated extensively on the environment, clean air, clean water, and endangered species?

You may be surprised to learn that Congress' power to regulate

11

commerce among the several states is claimed in order to authorize environmental legislation. Migratory ducks fly across a state line and land on seasonal ponds located on private property. Is that "commerce among the several states" to you? It is to Congress and the courts. Duck hunters buy guns and shells that are shipped across state lines, so the ducks and the seasonal ponds on which they land "affect" interstate commerce. And so it follows, as night follows day, that the federal government has the constitutional power to tell the owners of the seasonal ponds what they may or may not do with their "ponds." You don't get it? I have sympathy with your frustration, but that is the interpretation of the Clean Water Act in the states of Alaska, Arizona, California, Hawaii, Idaho, Montana, Nevada, Oregon, and Washington. (See *Leslie Salt Company v. United States* [1995] [Ninth Circuit] 55 F3d 1388.)

How does Congress get from commerce to clean water to migratory ducks on seasonal ponds? Well, somewhat like the schoolboy who had read up on worms for the biology exam, and found the question was about the elephant. The boy took one look—and nearly despaired— but then he saw his way: The elephant has a long trunk. This trunk is shaped like a big worm. There are twelve classes of worms. The first class is the long thin worms, the second class is the short fat worms, and so on.

Is it still a government of laws, and not of men's whims, if our representatives read the Constitution in this manner? The answer—and the responsibility for it—is ours.

What Congress really has done is to pretend that the Constitution provides that Congress shall have power to regulate water, air, plants and wildlife throughout the United States, no holds barred.

We need to protect the physical environment, but don't we also need to protect our system of government, a federal union, based on the Constitution?

The Supreme Court too, from time to time, has in effect amended the Constitution. Please understand, though, that the justices of the Supreme Court don't conspire to amend the Constitution. They are moved to their decisions by that old English system of legal reasoning by analogy to precedent which the British planted in the Thirteen Colonies. Long lists of prior decisions by the Court channel their thinking toward the decisions they reach (see Chapter II).

I read every decision of the Supreme Court as it is published. The law professors and the media like to classify the justices as liberal, conservative, pro-labor, pro-business, and so on. You should take that stuff with a grain of salt. Most of the time the justices conscientiously struggle to fit the new cases before them with the long lists of prior decisions. Of course they often disagree violently with each other about the proper way to reconcile a pending case with the past cases. But they don't just sit down and "vote"—liberal, conservative, pro-labor, pro-business, or whatever. Sure, every justice on the Court has a different personal philosophy which will influence, or even control, his or her reading of the precedents. But each one struggles to the best of their ability to be true to the law as he or she understands it. Yet one might say that sometimes that old English system of legal reasoning puts blinders on them, so they can't look sideways. And sometimes the fabric that binds a new holding to precedent and to the Constitution becomes very thin. That is why the citizens need to have the means of quickly correcting judicial amendments to the Constitution.

In this book I try to deal with the Court as an institution, not as an assemblage of individuals; therefore I do not refer to any living justice by name. Occasionally I mention the names of deceased justices who have become historical figures.

Why do I say the Court is "amending" the Constitution rather than "interpreting" it in the light of modern experience when it creates new meaning for some key phrases of the Constitution (for example, "due process of law")? Well, there is a difference between interpreting the old words to get to their substance, as we have seen with "army" and "navy," and adding new substance under the guise of interpretation. The Court itself has recognized this difference when dealing with congressional legislation: "Congress does not enforce a constitutional right by changing what the right is" (*City of Boerne v. Flores* [1997] 521 US 507, 138 L Ed 2d 624, at 638–639, 117 S Ct 2157).

The line is difficult to draw, the Court allowed, but "the distinction exists and must be observed."

For an example, let us take a close look at the Constitution's command that "nor shall any State deprive any person of life, liberty, or property, without due process of law…" (Fourteenth Amendment, Section 1). To deprive means to take away, as these examples show:

- deprived of life—a death sentence for murder

- deprived of liberty—a sentence to a term of imprisonment for robbery
- deprived of property—the government takes some land you own to build a highway over it

The government may not do any of the above "without due process of law," but if the government has followed due process of law, it may carry out a death sentence, it may imprison a robber, it may take your land for the highway.

So what is "due process of law?" Who makes laws? Congress and the state legislatures. Nobody else (with a limited exception for the courts, see Chapter II) is given the power to make laws, neither by the U.S. Constitution nor by the state constitutions.

Then what does "due process of law" mean in today's plain English?

As the first meaning for "due," the dictionary gives "immediately owed." As the second meaning it gives "owing, owed." As the third meaning it gives "owing or observed as a moral or natural right." As the fourth meaning it gives "rightful, proper, fitting." For "process" the dictionary also gives a number of meanings which come down to something which goes forward step by step through a period of time, such as "the whole course of the proceedings" in a legal action (*Random House Dictionary of the English Language*, Unabridged Edition, 1967). So "due process of law" means, in plain English, that the Constitutions, Federal and state, and the laws which Congress or the state legislatures have created, must be followed, step by step, in a rightful manner, as distinguished from the arbitrary whim of a sheriff or judge, before life, liberty or property may be taken away from you.

Thus "due process of law" refers to the process by which the law is *applied* to your case, not to the process by which law is *made*. "Due process of law" takes the law as it stands at the time. By a plain reading of today's English it is a command to the judges to apply the law to everybody "rightfully," or "as owed." So, when the judges say that the constitutional requirement of "due process of law" gives them the power not only to properly apply the procedures established by law, but also to create nonprocedural rights which previously did not exist, that's when they are amending the Constitution to, in effect, read "nor shall any State deprive any person of life, liberty, or property, without due _____ law."

And the Supreme Court, having the last word on what the Constitution means, decides what law is "due."

Some of the judicial or congressional amendments to the Constitution were desired by the majority of the citizens. We accept them, particularly those which might be called our judicial "Bill of Individual Liberties" (see Chapter II). But the citizens need the practical means to correct those amendments which we do not and need not accept.

One important example is abortion. Abortion is no business of the United States federal government. When you read the words "nor shall any State deprive any person of life, liberty, or property, without due process of law" (Fourteenth Amendment, Section 1), do they tell you that the federal government is thereby given power to legislate about abortion, and to override state laws that deal with abortion?

Power over the laws of inheritance, marriage, adoption, legitimacy, spousal and child support, divorce, incest, abortion and similar matters has always been with the states and was never intended to be delegated to the federal government. If "due process of law" gives the Court power to decide when abortion is lawful, then that phrase logically gives the Court also power to decide when persons may marry, when they may dissolve a marriage, when they may adopt children, and so forth.

Besides "due process of law," the other alleged source for this new power of the Court are the words: "The enumeration in the Constitution, of certain rights, shall not be construed to deny or disparage others retained by the people" (Ninth Amendment).

What does that mean? It means that there is a list of rights of the people in the federal Constitution, known as the Bill of Rights (First through Tenth Amendments), which the federal government must respect, such as free exercise of religion, freedom of speech, right to bear arms, right to be secure from unreasonable searches and seizures, right to jury trial, right to counsel, and so on.

The Ninth Amendment says that the federal government may not argue that the people have no other rights, because such other rights are not listed in the Constitution (or its Amendments). But is it sensible to read these words as giving power to the Court to add a right to abortion to the list of rights protected by the Constitution? The people have expressed through their state legislatures that abortion, if it is a "right" at all, is subject to regulation by the majority of the people in each state, through their elected representatives.

By a fair reading of the Constitution, the agreement between all citizens, the phrase "rights retained by the people" does not mean that the Court, or the Congress, or the President have been given power to make rules about abortion. Congress may legislate about abortion in the District of Columbia. There it has "exclusive legislation." But that is the extent of it, by the text of the Constitution. As for the rights retained by the people, shouldn't it be the people who decide what's been retained?

How did we get to the point where Congress and the Court make rules about abortion? Well, in *Roe v. Wade* (1973) 410 US 113, 35 L Ed 2d 147, 93 S Ct 705, the *Court*, in effect, amended the Constitution by saying that the words "deprived of liberty without due process of law" mean that a woman is deprived of her liberty without "due process of law" when a duly elected state legislature by majority vote, following all the requirements of the regular legislative process, adopts a statute which prohibits or restricts abortion, and the state, through its duly elected executive attempts to enforce that statute in its own courts, following all the rules of due procedure.

Once the Court had said that the Constitution prevents states from prohibiting or "unduly" restricting abortion, then Congress felt it too could make rules about abortion.

This is not the first time the Court has made a mistake. Back in 1857, for example, in the *Dred Scott* case, the Court said that Congress had no power to prohibit slavery in the territories of the United States, despite the fact that the Constitution expressly gives Congress the power to "make all needful Rules and Regulations respecting the Territory ... belonging to the United States" (Article IV, Section 3, Clause 2).

The Court said Congress could not make rules which prevented slaveholders from bringing their "property" into the territories, because that would deprive the slaveholders of their property without "due process of law." But the Constitution did not say that slaves were property, and it even authorized Congress to prohibit, after 1807, the migration or importation of slaves into any of the states (Article I, Section 9). Since Congress had that power as to the States, and had power to make all needful rules for the territories, how could the Court hold that nevertheless Congress could not forbid slavery in the territories? It did it by reading the words "deprived of property without due process of law" not only as referring to the requirement of regular procedure, but as creating a constitutional right to own slaves anywhere and to take them wherever one pleases. In effect, this decision was an amendment to the Constitution, not approved by the citizens, which made the Constitution read: "The Congress shall have Power to ... make all needful Rules and Regulations respecting the Territory ... belonging to the United States [Article IV, Section 3, Clause 2], *except rules and regulations concerning the migration or importation of slaves* [emphasis added]" (see *Dred Scott v. Sanford* [1857] 60 US [19 How.] 393, at 620 [dissenting opinion]; 15 L Ed 691. Also, William H. Rehnquist, *The Supreme Court: How It Was, How It Is* New York: William Morrow, 1987, p. 133–145, for the *Dred Scott* case generally).

As you well know, it took 600,000 dead soldiers, blue and gray, to overrule this decision of the Court, but the citizens did overrule it.

I have suggested that the Court's abortion ruling was a mistake, like the Court's *Dred Scott* ruling. How can I justify this suggestion? All that needs to be said at this point is that American citizens have killed fellow citizens over the issue, in more than one isolated instance. We have had our John Browns of abortion. The issue remains deeply divisive.

Other mistaken rulings the Court overruled itself, after recognizing it had made a mistake. For example, for many years the Court invalidated state laws which limited working hours and regulated working conditions. The Court said that workers were deprived of their liberty without due process of law, if the states interfered with how many hours the workers could contractually "agree" to work on each day. It was part of the worker's liberty to "agree" to work 12 hours a day. This was another court amendment to the Constitution. It was called "freedom of contract." Eventually, after many years of social strife, the Court realized its error and removed the "constitutional" obstacles to legislative regulation of working hours and conditions (see generally: Archibald Cox, *The Court and the Constitution*, Boston: Houghton Mifflin, 1987, p. 129–137. Rehnquist, *The Supreme Court*, p. 205–214).

But today "due process of law" and possibly "equal protection of the laws" still tempt court amendments to the Constitution. It is settled doctrine of the Supreme Court that "due process of law" means "more than fair process" (*Washington v. Glucksburg* [1997] 521 US 702, 138 L Ed 2d 772, at 787, 117 S Ct 2258). In other words the Court still makes the Constitution read "nor shall any State deprive any person of life, liberty, or property, without due ____ law" with the Court stating what "due law" is. (See also: *Troxel v. Granville* (2000) 530 US 57, 147 L Ed 2d 49, 120 S Ct 2054).

The only way we, the citizens, could effectively rein in this power would be by giving ourselves a procedure for exercising our power to directly correct interpretations of the Constitution, by ballot. This would leave untouched the existing amendment provisions of the Constitution (Article V) which are too time consuming for the occasional small corrections needed to rein in the president, Congress or the Court, as the case may be.

Once we, the citizens, have amended the Constitution to give us the practical means to make corrective interpretations by ballot, we would probably have to use this new method very rarely. The mere possibility that we might correct by ballot acts of Congress, executive orders, decisions of the Supreme Court, or agency regulations that go beyond the Constitution as we read it would cause all branches of our government to proceed more cautiously.

Of course, if we, the citizens, should proceed to petition for a constitutional amendment giving us a procedure to correct by ballot misinterpretations of the Constitution, be prepared to meet a torrent of media, academic and political pundit howls. (This one is for connoisseurs of mixed metaphors.) Saying, or howling, or whining, that it will be the end of the Constitution if acts of Congress or decisions of the Supreme Court, and so forth, can be corrected directly by the citizens.

Close your ears to these noises and persist! If you get a chance to talk with the howlers, ask them how they square their position with "government of the people, by the people, for the people." Their objection that we, the citizens, cannot be entrusted with directly correcting misinterpretations of our Constitution has only one possible basis in reason: namely, that we are too ignorant, careless, emotional, illiterate, lazy and incompetent to run our own government; that we should leave this to the "elite," the people who "know," the people who brought us the ruin of the family by permissiveness and ill-conceived welfare.

So there's a first taste of the problem. Next we can go over the details, chapter by chapter, to look at some more examples of informal amendments, by Congress or the Court, that may need correction. It will be up to us to act on this information.

Nothing immediately noticeable will happen if we don't act. The

Constitution, that lovable old historic document, will become pure history. It will be there, it will be revered, and it will be ignored. Congress will continue to legislate as it pleases on anything under the sun, except where it is cowed into submission by the threat of a presidential veto.

So from year to year this country will slide further into being ruled by the president, assisted by a Congress with unlimited powers of legislation. The president will continue to kowtow to that collection of warlords, robber barons, dictators, kings, and more or less democratically elected governments—all voting equally in the assembly—known as the United Nations.

But this country will survive in good shape for a long time. It is too big, too good, and too tough to go down the drain quickly. After the one man rule of the Roman empire was started, under the guise that the emperor was only the first man in the senate, the empire still lasted for hundreds of years.

So the sky is not going to fall, if we do nothing about the Constitution. But American self-government is likely to become a shadow of its former self—we will cease to govern ourselves under a written constitution.

Chapter I

The Expansion of the Powers of Congress

Over the years, Congress has informally amended the Commerce Clause and the Taxing for the General Welfare Clause of the Constitution to turn itself into a legislature of almost unlimited powers.

The Constitution has seven articles. Briefly stated, they are:

- Article I—creates Congress, lists the basic powers given to Congress, and lists powers prohibited to Congress and the states.
- Article II—creates the presidency and lists the president's powers.
- Article III—creates the United States Supreme Court, gives Congress the power to create federal courts below the Supreme Court, and describes what kind of cases may be decided by the federal courts.
- Article IV—gives some rules for relations between the states and for admitting new states, and gives Congress complete power over "the territory or other property belonging to the United States."
- Article V—provides the mechanism for amending the Constitution.
- Article VI—makes the new federal government responsible for the debts incurred during the Revolutionary War, and provides that the Constitution is the "supreme law of the land" that must be followed and supported by all judges, legislators, and government officials, state and federal.
- Article VII—provides rules for the ratification of the Constitution; these are of purely historical interest today, since the Constitution was ratified by all thirteen states.

The basic powers of Congress are listed in Article I of the Constitution. Additional powers are stated in other articles and in some of the amendments. (Twenty-seven amendments were added to the original seven articles.) We should have a quick look at all these specified powers of Congress before focusing on those powers that, nowadays, seem to have been extended beyond the reasonable meaning of the words by which they are expressed.

——— THE ARTICLES ———

Let us go through the Constitution's articles and amendments in sequence, to find the powers expressly given to Congress:

Article I

Section 2

CLAUSE 3: Congress has the power to direct an "actual enumeration" of the population of the United States every ten years (the Census).

CLAUSE 5: The House of Representatives has the power to start impeachment proceedings.

Section 3

CLAUSE 6: The Senate has the power to try impeachments.

Section 4

With one exception, Congress has the power to change state laws that provide for the times, places, and manner of holding elections for U.S. Senators and Congressmen, and Congress has power to set the day on which the required annual assembly of Congress begins.

Section 8

Congress has the power:

CLAUSE 1: "To lay and collect Taxes ... to pay the Debts and provide for the common Defence and general Welfare of the United States..." (this is one of the great expansive clauses on which modern big government rests).

CLAUSE 2: "To borrow Money on the credit of the United States."

CLAUSE 3: "To regulate Commerce with foreign Nations, and among the several States..." (this is the second great expansive clause on which modern big government is built).

CLAUSE 4: to create uniform laws on bankruptcy and naturalization.

CLAUSE 5: to regulate the currency and fix weights and measures.

CLAUSE 6: to punish counterfeiting of money and securities.

CLAUSE 7: "To establish Post Offices and post Roads."

CLAUSE 8: to enact patent and copyright laws.

CLAUSE 9: to create the lower federal courts.

CLAUSE 10: to punish crimes on the high seas and offenses against the law of nations.

CLAUSE 11: "To declare War."

CLAUSE 12: "To raise and support Armies."

CLAUSE 13: "To provide and maintain a Navy."

CLAUSE 14: to regulate the land and naval forces.

CLAUSE 15: "To provide for calling forth the Militia..." (in case of war, etc.).

CLAUSE 16: to regulate the militia, except that the states appoint the officers.

CLAUSE 17: to have "exclusive Legislation" over the District of Columbia and over federal forts, dockyards, and so on.

CLAUSE 18: "To make all Laws which shall be necessary and proper for carrying into Execution the foregoing Powers, and all other Powers vested by this Constitution in the Government of the United States, or in any Department or Officer thereof."

Section 9

CLAUSE 1: Congress has the power to impose a tax or duty on the importation of slaves and to prohibit it from 1808 onwards.

CLAUSE 2: When the public safety, in cases of rebellion or invasion, requires it, Congress may suspend "The Privilege of the Writ of Habeas Corpus."

CLAUSE 8: Congress has the power to consent to an officeholder of the United States receiving a "present, Emolument, Office, or Title" from a foreign power.

Section 10

CLAUSE 2: Congress has the power to consent to a state's laying a duty on imports or exports, under limited circumstances.

CLAUSE 3: Congress has the power to consent to a state's taking steps, under limited circumstances, that affect foreign relations.

Article II

Section 1 (Partially superseded by the Twentieth Amendment.) Congress has certain powers relating to presidential elections and presidential succession.

Section 2

CLAUSE 2: The Senate has the power of "Advice and Consent" regarding treaties with foreign powers and appointment of ambassadors, Supreme Court "Judges," and other important federal officeholders.

Congress has the power to give to the president, the courts, and the "Heads of Departments" the power to appoint "Inferior Officers."

Article III

Section 2

CLAUSE 3: Congress has the power to determine the place of trial for crimes not committed within a state.

Section 3

With some limitations, Congress has the power to "declare the Punishment of Treason."

Article IV

Section 1

Congress "may by general Laws prescribe the Manner in which" official acts of one state may be proven in another state.

Section 3

CLAUSE 1: With some limitations, Congress has the power to admit new states to the Union.

CLAUSE 2: Congress has the power "to dispose of and make all needful Rules and Regulations respecting the Territory or other Property belonging to the United States."

Article V

Congress has the power, by two-thirds vote, and with some limitations, to propose amendments to the Constitution.

——— THE AMENDMENTS ———

The additional powers given to Congress by some of the 27 amendments fall into three groups: powers to "enforce" various amendments, the income tax power, powers connected with the election and replacement of the president and the vice President.

1) Congress has the power to "enforce" the following amendments "by appropriate legislation":

Thirteenth Amendment (Slavery)

Fourteenth Amendment (Civil Rights)

Fifteenth Amendment (Voting discrimination based on color, race, previous condition of servitude)

Nineteenth Amendment (Voting discrimination based on sex)

Twenty-third Amendment (Participation of the District of Columbia in presidential elections)

Twenty-fourth Amendment (Voting discrimination based on failure to pay "any poll tax or other tax")

Twenty-sixth Amendment (Right to vote when eighteen or older).

2) Congress, by the Sixteenth Amendment, has the power to lay and collect the income tax, without apportionment among the states.

3) Congress, by the Twelfth Amendment, has certain powers in connection with the election of the president and vice president.

Twentieth Amendment: Congress has certain powers in connection with the death of the president-elect and vice president–elect, and provision for an acting president.

Twenty-fifth Amendment: Congress has certain powers in connection with the death, resignation or removal of the President or Vice President.

These then, are the legislative powers expressly delegated to Congress found in the original seven articles of the Constitution and the 27 amendments.

The power "to make all Laws which shall be necessary and proper" (Article I, Section 8, Clause 18) applies to all powers given to Congress, to make them effective. But any necessary and proper law must relate to a power expressly given to Congress.

So far the Framers were in agreement, but, as we shall see further on, they disagreed within a year after the new United States government was formed in 1789 over how broadly or how narrowly the word "necessary" should be interpreted.

In the list above there is no mention of power over urban housing, education, caring for the disabled, air, water (other than water connected with navigation, which is part of commerce), the arts, endangered species habitat on private land outside federal property, speed limits on state roads, and so on.

So now to see how power over these unlisted subjects is attempted to be justified, we need to have a look at the provisions in the Constitution that are claimed today to give Congress power over everything, clauses that you might call the "big government clauses."

Article I

Section 8

CLAUSE 1: The power "To lay and collect Taxes ... to pay the Debts and provide for the common Defence and general Welfare of the United States" (Taxing for the General Welfare Clause).

CLAUSE 3: The power "To regulate Commerce with foreign Nations, and among the several States..." (Commerce Clause).

CLAUSE 18: The power "to make all Laws which shall be necessary and proper for carrying into Execution the foregoing Powers, and all other Powers vested by this Constitution in the Government of the United States, or in any Department or officer thereof" (Necessary and Proper Clause).

As I mentioned before, we, the citizens, have to make up our minds what these provisions of the Constitution shall mean today, because as we shall see in the following the framers had differing opinions about the meaning of these provisions from the start. There is no single settled original meaning that could bind us.

CLAUSE 1. As you look at this clause, you see immediately that it can be read in several ways:

FIRST VERSION: Congress shall have power to lay and collect taxes to pay the debts and provide for the common defense and general welfare of the United States (but only as specified in Clauses 2 through 18 following).

SECOND VERSION: Congress shall have power to lay and collect taxes to pay the debts and provide for the common defense and general welfare of the United States (without being limited to Clauses 2 through 18 following).

THIRD VERSION: Congress shall have power (for all of the following in addition to Clauses 2 through 18):

(1) to lay and collect taxes, (2) to pay the debts of the United States, (3) to provide for the common defense of the United States, and (4) (to provide for the) general welfare of the United States.

Which of the three versions is the true meaning of the Constitution? This problem has been with us from the beginning of the Republic.

In 1788, before the Constitution had even been adopted, a publicist writing under the name of "Brutus" predicted the system we very nearly have today:

> This will certainly give the first clause in [Article I, Section 8] a construction which I confess I think the most natural and grammatical one, to authorize the Congress to do any thing which in their judgment will tend to provide for the general welfare, and this amounts to the same thing as general and unlimited powers of legislation in all cases [Kurland, Vol. 4, p. 237, No. 20 (1788)].

President Washington took the oath of office for his first term on April 30, 1789. The Constitution was ratified by the last of the thirteen states on May 29, 1790 (Rhode Island).

On February 2, 1791, James Madison (a leading member of the framing convention, elected to the First Congress) stated that the first version was the true meaning. The power given was only the power to tax, and as regards the terms "common Defence and general Welfare," Madison said, "The power as to these general purposes, was limited to acts laying taxes for them; and the general purposes themselves were limited and explained by the particular enumeration subjoined" (Kurland, Vol. 2, p. 446, No. 20 [1791]).

This "particular enumeration" is clauses 2 through 18 of Section 8, of Article I, the basic list of congressional powers.

To interpret these terms in any other way would, continued Madison, "give to Congress an unlimited power; would render nugatory the enumeration of particular powers; would supercede [sic] all the powers reserved to the state governments."

You have just labored through the 35 clauses of the original Constitution which list the powers given to Congress. It would seem obvious that Madison must have been right. Who would carefully negotiate 35 clauses of limited powers, if they wanted Congress to have unlimited powers of legislation?

Yet on December 5, 1791, Alexander Hamilton (secretary of the treasury in Washington's administration) stated that the second version was the true meaning. The power given, Hamilton said, was to tax for any purpose Congress considered to be for the "general Welfare." For example, "the general Interests of *learning* of *Agriculture* of *Manufactures* and of *Commerce* are within the sphere of the national Councils *as far as regards an application of Money.*"

The only limitation was that "the object to which an appropriation of money is to be made be *General* and not *local*; its operation extending in fact, or by possibility, throughout the Union, and not being confined to a particular spot" (Kurland, Vol. 2, p. 447, No. 21 [1791]).

So clauses 2 through 18, in Hamilton's view, were not limitations on the objects for which federal tax money could be spent.

Hamilton felt there could be no objection to reading the Constitution this way, because

> "a power to appropriate money with this latitude which is granted too in *express terms* would not carry a power to do any other thing, not authorized by the Constitution, either expressly or by fair implication." It would just be a power to *appropriate money* for what Congress considered to be the general welfare and would *not* be "a power to do whatever else should appear to Congress conducive to the General Welfare" [Kurland, Vol. 2, p. 446–447, No. 21 (1791)].

Did Hamilton really believe that the federal government would give away tax money for matters of "general welfare," without strings attached ? With the benefit of hindsight we know better. Just one example: highway funds conditioned on enacting federal billboard controls, speed limits and drinking age. (Title 23 of the *United States Code Annotated*, Sections 131, 154, and 158.)

The two interpretations, Madison's and Hamilton's, highlight the issues on which the founders soon divided themselves into two parties: the Federalists, led by Hamilton, standing for the broad, liberal interpretation of the Constitution, for "big government" as it were; and the Republicans, headed by Jefferson and Madison, who stood for a more restrained interpretation of the Constitution. The dispute over the scope of the tax and general welfare provisions (Article I, Section 8, Clause 1) flared up in the context of "internal improvements," that is roads, canals, harbors, lighthouses, to be paid for with federal tax money. As an example, James Madison at the end of his second term as president vetoed in 1817 a bill that earmarked certain federal revenues for extensive "internal improvements." (See *The Oxford History of the American People* by Samuel Eliot Morison, New York: Oxford University Press, 1965 [1972 reprint], p. 403.)

Thomas Jefferson applauded:

> it is almost the only landmark which now divides the federalists from the republicans, that Congress had not unlimited powers to provide for the general welfare, but were restrained to those specifically enumerated; and that, as it was never meant they should provide for that welfare but by the exercise of the enumerated powers, so it could not have been meant they should raise money for purposes which the enumeration did not place under their action; consequently, that the specification of powers is a limitation of the purposes for which they may raise money.

Jefferson hoped that Madison's veto of the internal improvement bill

> will settle forever the meaning of this phrase, which, by a mere grammatical quibble, has countenanced the General Government in a claim of universal power. For in the phrase "to lay taxes, to pay the debts and provide for the general welfare," it is a mere question of syntax, whether the two last infinitives are governed by the first or are distinct and co-ordinate powers; a question unequivocally decided by the exact definition of powers immediately following [Kurland, Vol. 2, p. 452, No. 25 (1817)].

History has gone the other way. Today Congress claims, or rather exercises, "universal power" as to what federal taxes may be used for, unrestrained by the enumerated powers. (See Chapters III, IV, IX.)

Think of Congress' carrot and stick approach in doling out federal money, on condition that state programs follow federal regulations. Citizens of a state can ill afford to pay federal taxes and then forgo return of (at least) some of these taxes by way of federal programs. So the states have little choice but to follow the federal dictates to get back money that, to a large extent, never should have left the state in the first place; money that was collected to do a job the federal government was not supposed to do in the first place.

The next of the great expansive clauses, the Commerce Clause (Article I, Section 8, Clause 3), also gave rise to opposing views. Did "commerce" include navigation? Did it include manufacture? And was there a line between "commerce ... among the several states" and commerce entirely within a state? Chief Justice John Marshall (on the Court 1801–1835), the head of what Jefferson called the "federalist" judiciary (Kurland, Vol. 3, p. 261, No. 16), observed in 1824 that, yes, "all America understands ... the word 'commerce' to comprehend navigation," and as to the interstate and in-state question, that "the completely internal commerce of a State ... may be considered as reserved for the State itself" (Kurland, Vol. 2, p. 499, No. 16). But there was no bright line between interstate and in-state. In 1827 Marshall phrased it thus: "the distinction exists and must be marked as the cases arise. Till they do arise, it might be premature to state any rule as being universal in its application" (Kurland, Vol. 2, p. 511, No. 17 [1827]).

Cases did arise, over the years, up to the ducks flying across state-lines and landing on private vernal ponds (see Introduction and Ch. VII).

In modern constitutional doctrine the phrase "affecting commerce" has become crucial. Congress is rarely restricted by the Court, when it claims that an activity "affects commerce" (see Chapters VI, VII, VIII).

This development was foreseen with singular accuracy by Justice Joseph Story (a Justice of the Supreme Court from 1811 to 1845):

> Are not commerce and manufacture as distinct, as commerce and agriculture? If they are, how can a power to regulate one arise from a power to regulate the other? It is true, that commerce and manufactures are ... intimately connected with each other.... But ... the point in controversy ... is, whether congress has a right to regulate that, which is not committed to it [manufacture], under a power which is committed to it [commerce], simply because there is ... an intimate connexion [sic] between the powers. If this were admitted, the enumeration of the powers of congress would be wholly unnecessary and nugatory. Agriculture, colonies, capital, machinery, the wages of labour, the profits of stock, the rents of land, the punctual performance of contracts, and the diffusion of knowledge would all be within the scope of the power; for all of them bear an intimate relation to commerce. The result would be, that the powers of congress would embrace the widest extent of legislative functions, to the utter demolition of all constitutional boundaries between the state and national governments [Kurland, Vol. 2, p. 524, No. 22 (1833)].

We have, today, not quite reached that point, but we are getting close to it.

The third clause on which the overexpansion of federal power rests, in conjunction with the two great expansive clauses, is the Necessary and Proper Clause (Article I, Section 8, Clause 18).

Early on, Jefferson and Hamilton split over the interpretation of the word "necessary" in the dispute over the "Bank of the United States," which had been proposed by Hamilton. In 1791, President Washington asked Jefferson, then his secretary of state, and Hamilton, his secretary of the treasury, for a written opinion about the constitutionality of the proposed bill for incorporating a "Bank of the United States."

Jefferson argued that the bank was not "necessary" for performing Congress' function of collecting taxes, but was merely convenient. If the "necessary and proper" clause were to be construed this broadly, "It would reduce the whole instrument [the Constitution] to a single phrase, that of instituting a Congress with power to do whatever would be for the good of the U.S. and as they would be the sole judges of the good or evil, it would be also a power to do whatever evil they pleased" (Kurland, Vol. 3, p. 246, No. 10 [1791]).

Madison had opposed the bill in Congress on the same grounds as Jefferson. (Kurland, Vol. 3, p. 244, No. 9 [1791].)

Hamilton asserted that

> neither the grammatical nor popular sense of the term requires that construction. According to both, *necessary* often means no more than *needful, requisite, incidental, useful,* or *conducive to.* It is a common mode of expression to say, that it is necessary for a government or a person to do this or that thing, when nothing more is intended or understood, than that the interests of the government or person require, or will be promoted, by the doing of this or that thing.

To understand the word as Jefferson does "would be to give it the same force as if the word *absolutely* or *indispensably* had been prefixed to it" (Kurland, Vol. 3, p. 249, No. 11 [1791]).

In Hamilton's opinion, the power to "erect corporations," though not expressly delegated, was nevertheless implied to Congress as a means to carry into execution the powers expressly delegated to it. The criterion by which to judge whether a power is "necessary and proper," Hamilton said,

> is the *end*, to which the measure relates as a *mean*. If the end be clearly comprehended within any of the specified powers, and if the measure

have an obvious relation to that end, and is not forbidden by any particular provision of the constitution—it may safely be deemed to come within the compass of the national authority" [Kurland, Vol. 3, p. 250, No. 11 (1791)].

Hamilton's opinion satisfied President Washington who did not veto the bill.

But for forty years the argument swayed back and forth. In 1832 President Andrew Jackson vetoed legislation intended to renew and extend the bank's charter. Jackson answered the argument that the matter was settled by congressional precedent and by decision of the Supreme Court, by pointing out that while Congress had twice been in favor (1791 and 1816) it had also twice been against the bank (1811 and 1815). So the congressional precedents were equally for and against. As to the Supreme Court, Jackson said:

> The Congress, the Executive, and the Court must each for itself be guided by its own opinion of the Constitution.... The authority of the Supreme Court must not, therefore, be permitted to control the Congress or the Executive when acting in their legislative capacities, but to have only such influence as the force of their reasoning may deserve [Kurland, Vol. 3, p. 263, No. 20].

This echoed Jefferson's opinion, expressed years earlier, that the three departments of government were coordinate and independent, "that they might check and balance one another," and that the Constitution did not give to one of them [the Court]

> the right to prescribe rules for the government of the others, and to that one too, which is unelected by, and independent of the nation ... each department is truly independent of the others, and has an equal right to decide for itself what is the meaning of the constitution in the cases submitted to its action; and especially, where it is to act ultimately and without appeal" [Kurland, Vol. 3, p. 261, No. 16 (1819)].

And it foreshadowed Lincoln's similar opinion, announced in his first inaugural address:

> if the policy of the Government upon vital questions affecting the whole people is to be irrevocably fixed by decisions of the Supreme Court, the instant they are made in ordinary litigation between parties in personal actions the people will have ceased to be their own

rulers, having to that extent practically resigned their Government into the hands of that eminent tribunal.

More about this problem in the next chapter.

Jackson, in his veto message, went item by item through the bill, pointing out provisions that were not necessary for the bank to carry out the function of assisting Congress in collecting taxes; for example, making the bank a monopoly, exempting foreign shareholders of the bank from all state and federal taxes, or indirectly giving alien shareholders title to real property located in the United States.

So, again, we see that the Framers from the beginning disagreed about the proper scope of this clause, giving us no single "Framers' intent" as potentially authoritative guidance.

Therefore, each generation of citizens will have to make up their mind what these clauses, or any other clauses of the Constitution, shall mean.

Madison, after observing the tug-of-war over the proper reading of the Constitution for some forty years, observed in 1831 that the Constitution

> is read by some as if it were a Constitution for a single Govt. with powers co-extensive with the general welfare, and by others interpreted as if it were an ordinary statute, and with the strictness almost of a penal one. Between these adverse constructions an intermediate course must be the true one, and it is hoped that it will finally if not otherwise settled be prescribed by an amendment of the Constitution [Kurland, Vol. 3, p. 262, No. 19 (1831)].

As of today, we do not have such an amendment.

The tug-of-war continued for a hundred years from the time of Madison's quoted comment to the New Deal era, at which time, after a last victory for Jefferson's and Madison's views, big government won decisively.

In the emergency of the Great Depression, President Franklin Roosevelt, supported by the majority of Congress and of the voters, attempted to stabilize the economy by imposing through various Acts of Congress, including the National Recovery Act of 1933, minimum wages, maximum hours, minimum prices, and limits on agricultural production to increase prices for agricultural commodities. Roosevelt's program was duly challenged in the courts.

In *Schechter Poultry Corporation v. United States* (1935) 295 U.S.

495, 79 L Ed 1570, 55 S Ct 837, the Supreme Court held the National Recovery Act of 1933 to be unconstitutional, as exceeding Congress' power under the Commerce Clause, when applied to intrastate transactions. Schechter was a poultry wholesaler in New York City that bought poultry shipped into the state from other states, but sold only to local retailers. The government asserted that hour and wage provisions decreed under the National Recovery Act applied to Schechter's slaughterhouse in Brooklyn because the chickens were still in the "flow" or "current" of interstate commerce. But the Court stayed with the plain meaning of the Constitution. "Among the several states" does not mean *within one state*: "So far as the poultry here in question is concerned, the flow in interstate commerce had ceased. The poultry had come to a permanent rest within the State" (295 US at p. 543).

As to the government's argument that the hours and wages of Schechter's employees affected Schechter's prices, and that these in turn affected prices in interstate commerce, the Court said

> the distinction between direct and indirect effects of intra-state transactions upon interstate commerce must be recognized as a fundamental one, essential to the maintenance of our constitutional system. Otherwise ... there would be virtually no limit to the federal power and for all practical purposes we should have a completely centralized government [295 US at p. 548].

and further, echoing Jefferson and Madison,

> the authority of the federal government may not be pushed to such an extreme as to destroy the distinction, which the commerce clause itself establishes, between commerce "among the several states" and the internal concerns of a State [295 US at p. 550].

The Court insisted that "the recuperative efforts of the federal government must be made in a manner consistent with the authority granted by the Constitution" (295 US at p.550). The Court was unanimous.

The *Schechter* case triggered public discussion of amending the Constitution to give Congress the powers over wages, hours and prices it had claimed in the National Recovery Act. (See for example 79 *Congressional Record* 104, 1935.) But no amendment was adopted.

A year later, in *Carter v. Carter Coal Company* (1936) 298 US 238, 80 L Ed 1160, 56 S Ct 855, the Court again read the Commerce Clause, in its common sense plain words, echoing Justice Story's "Are not commerce and manufacture as distinct, as commerce and agriculture?" The

Act of Congress in question declared that the production and distribution of bituminous coal "bear upon and directly affect its interstate commerce" and on this basis gave Congress power under the Commerce Clause to impose wage, hour and price regulation on the coal industry. The Court said,

> commerce succeeds to manufacture, and is not a part of it... Mining brings the subject matter of commerce into existence. Commerce disposes of it.... Extraction of coal from the mine is the aim and the completed result of local activities [298 US at pp. 300, 304, 303].

Since the wage and hour regulations of the act "primarily fall[s] upon production and not upon commerce," and since "such effect as they may have upon commerce, however extensive it may be, is secondary and indirect," the wage and hour regulations could not be upheld as an exercise of the power to regulate commerce among the several states.

As we shall see, *Schechter*, *Carter*, and a few similar cases were the last stand of the traditional, plain words, reading of the Commerce Clause.

In 1936, besides the Commerce Clause, the Taxing for the General Welfare Clause also became an issue. In *United States v. Butler* (1936) 297 US 1, 80 L Ed 477, 56 S Ct 312, the constitutionality of the Agricultural Adjustment Act of 1933 was challenged. The main feature of the act was a tax, collected from the first processors of agricultural commodities, and used to pay farmers for reducing their production. The government argued that the act was within Congress' power under the Taxing for the General Welfare Clause. The Court seemingly agreed with Hamilton's view that the clause was not limited by the list of powers in Article I, Section 8, which follow the clause, but held that the clause, nevertheless, was subject to limitations:

> We are not now required to ascertain the scope of the phrase "general welfare of the United States" or to determine whether an appropriation in aid of agriculture falls within it. Wholly apart from that question, another principle embedded in our Constitution prohibits the enforcement.... The act invades the reserved rights of the states. It is a statutory plan to regulate and control agricultural production, a matter beyond the powers delegated to the federal government [297 US at p. 68].

How do you know which powers were delegated? You go to the list in Article I, Section 8 (and to the other articles and sections I have summarized), don't you?

The Court held that such powers as are "not expressly granted, or reasonably to be implied from such as are conferred" are reserved to the states or the people by the Tenth Amendment. "The same proposition otherwise stated is that powers not granted are prohibited. None to regulate agricultural production is given, and therefore legislation by Congress for that purpose is forbidden" (297 US at p 68).

Three justices dissented.

So, despite the Court's apparent approval of Hamilton's view, the *Butler* case was a last victory of Jefferson's and Madison's view of the Taxing for the General Welfare power as limited to matters covered by enumerated delegated powers.

But President Franklin Roosevelt, supported by the majority of Congress and the majority of the voters, felt that the obstacle to the New Deal program was not the Constitution, but the way the old men on the Court read it. With the benefit of hindsight and free from the pressures of a great national emergency, we can now see that the Court in the cases discussed here merely adhered to the traditional, common sense plain words reading of the Constitution: Among the several states is not the same as within the United States. Our federal government is one of specific delegated powers, and powers not delegated stay with the people. Commerce is commerce, it is not manufacturing, or mining, or agriculture.

Thus the Constitution *needed to be changed* to accommodate the New Deal programs. The Roosevelt administration must have felt there was not time to make the change through the constitutional amendment process. So President Franklin Roosevelt conceived of a plan to nudge the Court towards a more accommodating reading of the Constitution, by adding, on every federal court, a younger justice or judge for every justice or judge who stayed on beyond retirement age. (See House of Representatives, Document No. 142, 75th Congress, First Session.) This is commonly referred to as the "court packing plan."

This plan turned out to be medicine too strong for Congress and the public to take. It was not enacted. But, for whatever reason, the majority of the Court now began to read the Constitution in a way that upheld the New Deal program.

In *National Labor Relations Board v. Jones & Laughlin Steel Corporation* (1937) 301 US 1, 81 L Ed 893, 57 S Ct 615, Justice Story's 1833 prediction came true:

machinery, the wages of labor... the rents of land ... would all be within the scope of the power; for all of them bear an *intimate relation* to commerce ... the powers of congress would embrace the widest extent of legislative function [Kurland, Vol. 2, p. 524, No. 22; emphasis added].

Upholding the National Labor Relations Act as a constitutional exercise of Congress' power under the Commerce Clause the Court said:

Because there may be but indirect and remote effects upon interstate commerce in connection with a host of local enterprises throughout the country, it does not follow that other industrial activities do not have such a close and *intimate relation* to interstate commerce as to make the presence of industrial strife a matter of the most urgent national concern [301 US at p. 41; emphasis added].

The steel company was "a completely integrated enterprise, owning and operating ore, coal, and limestone properties, lake and river transportation facilities and terminal railroads located at its manufacturing plants," the Court found.

[I]t presents in a most striking way the close and *intimate relation* which a manufacturing industry may have to interstate commerce and we have no doubt that Congress had constitutional authority to safeguard the right of respondent's [the steel company's] employees to self-organization and freedom in the choice of representatives for collective bargaining [301 US at p. 43; emphasis added].

The National Labor Relations Act, so upheld, relied on the phrase "affecting commerce" as giving Congress power over labor conditions at manufacturing plants. "Affecting commerce" was defined as meaning burdening or obstructing commerce or the free flow of commerce, or having led or tending to lead to a labor dispute burdening or obstructing commerce or the free flow of commerce" (301 US at p. 31). By the phrase "affecting commerce," as upheld by the Court, and subsequently expanded, Congress in effect amended the Commerce Clause to give itself power to regulate, in addition to commerce among the several states, any matter arguably affecting commerce from within a state.

This may be called the "New Deal Amendment." The text of the Constitution was "preserved," but the door to vast expansion of congressional power had been thrown open.

In 1803, St. George Tucker observed in a legal commentary on the Constitution:

> All governments have a natural tendency towards an increase, and assumption of power; and the administration of the federal government, has too frequently demonstrated, that the people of America are not exempt from this vice in their constitution. We have seen that parchment chains are not sufficient to correct this unhappy propensity; they are nevertheless, capable of producing the most salutary effects; for, when broken, they warn the people to change those perfidious agents, who dare violate them [Kurland, Vol. 3, p. 251, No. 12].

Nowadays we would say "paper chains." Ironically it was the majority of the people expressing themselves through the majority of Congress who in 1937 under the pressure of the continuing emergency broke the paper chains of the Commerce Clause. The emergency of the Great Depression was felt to make this necessary, without taking the time to amend the Constitution to fit the new circumstances.

If the purpose of a written constitution is to let the people mark down what their government may or may not do, then the words used in writing the Constitution must retain a meaning which every citizen can understand. That common sense meaning is lost when, for example, "commerce" also is made to mean "manufacture insofar as it affects commerce." It is a legal fiction that you regulate commerce when you legislate about labor conditions at a manufacturing plant. Lawyers are used to legal fictions. Legal fictions have great practical value. As the late Professor Karl Llewellyn observed, the country would be up in arms if the legislature were to enact a law compelling every person in its jurisdiction to get up one hour early in the summer, but the legal fiction that six o'clock on a summer morning is seven o'clock has only caused occasional grumbles.

But is it safe to use legal fictions with words of the Constitution? Do we not lose accountability?

Under the old Constitution, before the "New Deal Amendment," a constitutional amendment, the Eighteenth, was required to prohibit the manufacture, sale, or transportation of intoxicating liquors within the United States. If Prohibition had never been tried before the "New Deal Amendment," would not the argument be, now, that manufacture, sale and transportation of intoxicating liquors intimately affect commerce among the several states, and hence are subject to congressional "regulation," without a constitutional amendment?

The power to "regulate" commerce had for many years been interpreted as including the power to completely prohibit commerce in, for example, stolen goods, noxious articles, and kidnapped persons. Now with the "New Deal Amendment" providing that "commerce among the several states" includes manufacturing within a state, insofar as it "affects" interstate commerce, manufacturing could, in effect, be prohibited unless performed in accordance with rules made by Congress.

In *United States v. Darby* (1941) 312 US 100, 85 L Ed 609, 61 S Ct 451, the Court upheld the Fair Labor Standards Act of 1938. This act prescribes minimum wages and maximum hours for certain employees and prohibits the shipment in interstate commerce of goods produced for interstate commerce by employees whose wages and hours of employment do not conform to the requirements of the Act. The Court said that Congress is free to exclude from interstate commerce articles it may consider "injurious to the public health, morals or welfare" and this included goods produced under substandard labor conditions.

What if Congress should decide today that the manufacture, sale or transportation of cigarettes is "injurious to the public health ... or welfare" and prohibit cigarettes in interstate commerce? I mention this only to point out that the "New Deal Amendment" has drastically changed the Constitution.

What I have called the "New Deal Amendment" did not come about solely by one piece of legislation and one court decision upholding it. Besides the *Jones & Laughlin Steel Corporation* and *Darby* cases there were other cases interpreting various Acts of Congress in the light of the new Commerce Clause.

The high point of the new Constitution was reached in *Wickard v. Filburn* (1942) 317 US 111, 87 L Ed 122, 63 Sup Ct 82. Congress had defined the verb "to market" in the Agricultural Adjustment Act "so that as related to wheat in addition to its conventional meaning it also mean[t] to dispose of 'by feeding (in any form) to poultry or livestock which, or the products of which, are sold, bartered, or exchanged.'"

Federal regulation was thus extended "to production not intended in any part for commerce but wholly for consumption on the farm" (317 US at p. 118).

The Court upheld this regulation, as applied to a dairy farmer who had planted 11.9 acres of wheat in excess of the 11.1 acre allotment he had received. His excess yield was 239 bushels. The Court said:

> even if appellee's [the farmer's] activity be local and though it may
> not be regarded as commerce, it may still, whatever its nature, be
> reached by Congress if it exerts a substantial economic effect on inter-
> state commerce [317 US at p.125].

The Court found the "substantial economic effect" in the fact that all
wheat planted by farmers throughout the United States for their own consumption on their farms, taken together, substantially reduced the demand
for wheat in the United States, thereby lowering the price of wheat, contrary to Congress' intent of increasing the market price of wheat.

There are few activities by individuals living in this country, which,
all taken together, do not have a substantial economic effect on interstate commerce by this test. Consider, for example, homemade candy,
jams, jellies, fruit preserves, and cakes. But, as the Court said in *Wickard
v. Filburn*, "[t]hat an activity is of local character may help in a doubtful case to determine whether Congress intended to reach it" (317 US
at p.124). Congress' power "to reach it," however, is no longer in question under the "New Deal Amendment."

I want to stress again that the "New Deal Amendment," the new
Constitution, is not something imposed on the people by the Court.
To the contrary, one might fairly say that it was imposed on the Court
by the majority of the people expressing themselves through the majority of Congress and the Roosevelt administration. Under pressure from
the public the Court substituted legal fictions for the plain English
meaning of the word "commerce" and of the phrase "among the several
states," and thereby was able to uphold what amounted to an amendment of the Constitution by Congress' New Deal legislation.

In the sixty years since the New Deal, Congress has followed the
"natural tendency towards an increase, and assumption of power" of
which St. George Tucker wrote in 1803. Congress is as ready as ever to
break the "parchment chains" of the Constitution.

In the Gun-Free School Zones Act of 1990, Congress "regulated
commerce" by making it a federal offense to knowingly possess a firearm
in a school zone. Upon challenge to the constitutionality of the Act, in
United States v. Lopez (1995) 514 US 549, 131 L Ed 2d 626, 115 S Ct
1624, the Government argued before the Supreme Court that

> possession of a firearm in a local school zone does ... substantially
> affect interstate commerce [because it] may result in violent crime and
> that violent crime can be expected to affect the functioning of the

national economy in two ways. First, the costs of violent crime are substantial, and, through the mechanism of insurance, these costs are spread throughout the population.... Second, violent crime reduces the willingness of individuals to travel to areas within the country that are perceived to be unsafe. [In addition, the Government argued that] the presence of guns in schools poses a substantial threat to the education process by threatening the learning environment. A handicapped educational process, in turn, will result in a less productive citizenry. That, in turn, would have an adverse effect on the Nation's economic well-being [131 L Ed 2d at p. 640].

So, the government argued, Congress could rationally have concluded that gun possession in schools "substantially affects interstate commerce." The Court stood by the old Constitution: "The Constitution creates a Federal Government of enumerated powers."

The Commerce Clause, even after the New Deal expansion, is subject to outer limits. Under the government's "costs of crime" reasoning,

Congress could regulate not only all violent crime, but all activities that might lead to violent crime, regardless of how tenuously they relate to interstate commerce.... Similarly, under the Government's "national productivity" reasoning, Congress could regulate any activity that it found was related to the economic productivity of individual citizens: family law, including marriage, divorce and child custody ... for example. Under the theories that the Government presents ... it is difficult to perceive any limitation on federal power, even in areas such as criminal law enforcement or education where States historically have been sovereign. Thus, if we were to accept the Government's arguments, we are hard pressed to posit any activity by an individual that Congress is without power to regulate [131 L Ed 2d at p. 641].

The Court held that possession of a gun on school premises did not "substantially affect" interstate commerce and that congressional authority under the Commerce Clause is not "a general police power of the sort retained by the States."

But the Court was not unanimous. Four justices of the nine were willing to uphold the Act, under Congress' constitutional power "to regulate commerce among the several states," although even today the common meaning of "commerce" is: "an interchange of goods or commodities, esp. on a large scale between different countries ... or between parts of the same country" (*The Random House Dictionary of the English Language*, 1967); "an interchange of goods or commodities between different countries or between areas of the same country; trade" (*Random House Webster's College Dictionary*, 1997).

Thus the opinion of one Supreme Court justice stands between us and a Congress of unlimited powers under the Commerce Clause. (See also: *United States v. Morrison* (2000) 529 US n.a., 146 L. Ed 2d 658, at p. 675–677, 120 SA Ct n.a.)

As to the Taxing for the General Welfare Clause, which the Court nowadays describes as the "Spending Clause" or the "Spending Power," the Court has upheld a nearly unlimited power of Congress to place conditions on federal grants, which the States must obey to receive the money.

In *South Dakota v. Dole* (1987) 483 US 203, 97 L Ed 2d 171, 107 S Ct 2793, the state of South Dakota challenged an act of Congress that required a state to enact a drinking age limit of 21 years in order to receive its full share of federal highway funds. The Court said: "Here Congress has acted indirectly under its spending power to encourage uniformity in the States' drinking ages ... we find this legislative effort within constitutional bounds even if Congress may not regulate drinking ages directly" (97 L Ed 2d at p.177).

Let us pause for a moment and let this sink in. Congress may do indirectly through conditions on federal grants what it cannot do directly, since no power to do it was given to Congress by the Constitution? Sure, the Court seems to say, so long as "the financial inducement offered by Congress ... [is not] so coercive as to pass the point at which 'pressure turns into compulsion'" (97 L Ed 2d at p. 181).

Well, to whom is this financial inducement offered? To the states, and they are free to decline the federal money and keep their laws. But what of the people? The Tenth Amendment reserves "the powers not delegated to the United States ... to the States respectively, or to the people." Do the people have no right to expect that their national government will stay within its prescribed limits? Isn't it their tax money that, at least in part, comes back to them as a federal grant? They paid their federal taxes, expecting the money to be used for the federal purposes outlined in the Constitution and now it is offered back to them only if they change their state laws, laws which are not forbidden to them by the Constitution.

The only limits to conditions imposed under the Spending Power, the Court said, are that "the exercise of the spending power must be in pursuit of the 'general welfare,' that Congress must state the conditions "unambiguously," that they must be related "to the federal interest in particular national projects or programs," and that "the power may not

43

be used to induce the States to engage in activities that would themselves be unconstitutional."

The Court found that the drinking age condition "is directly related to one of the main purposes for which highway funds are expended—safe interstate travel" (97 L Ed 2d at p. 179).

Two Justices dissented. They argued that

> When Congress appropriates money to build a highway, it is entitled to insist that the highway be a safe one. But it is not entitled to insist as a condition of the use of highway funds that the State impose or change regulations in other areas of the State's social and economic life because of an attenuated or tangential relationship to highway use or safety. Indeed, if the rule were otherwise, the Congress could effectively regulate almost any area of the State's social, political, or economic life on the theory that use of the interstate transportation system is somehow enhanced [97 L Ed 2d at p. 183].

In the dissent's view, the drinking age condition was not reasonably related to interstate highway construction. The condition

> is over-inclusive because it stops teenagers from drinking even when they are not about to drive on interstate highways. It is under-inclusive because teenagers pose only a small part of the drunken driving problem in this Nation [97 L Ed 2d at p. 183].

The dissent concluded that the condition "is a regulation determining who shall be able to drink liquor. As such it is not justified by the Spending Power" (97 L Ed 2d at p. 185).

Remember Hamilton stating that "a power to appropriate money with this latitude ... would not carry a power to do any other thing, not authorized by the constitution."

Yet the Court held in *South Dakota v. Dole* that Congress could do indirectly by Spending Clause conditions what it had no power to do directly, namely, regulate the States' minimum drinking age laws.

Thus the Commerce Clause and the Spending Clause as interpreted by Congress (and, in part, by the Court) are now close to giving Congress unlimited power over what used to be state concerns. If we want to preserve our system of two governments, national and state, each responsible for its separate sphere of legislative action, both elected directly by the people and responsible directly to them, we will need to find Madison's "intermediate course." We may have to undo some of what Congress and the Court have done in the last fifty years, as will become apparent in later chapters.

Chapter II

The Expansion of
the Judicial Power

*Over the years the Court has informally amended the Constitution
and has created a Bill of Individual Liberties.*

The Constitution places the "judicial Power of the United States" in "one supreme Court, and in such inferior Courts as the Congress may from time to time ordain and establish" (Article III, Section 1).

The "judicial power" itself is not further described in the Constitution. The judges and lawyers who lived in the United States at the time the Constitution was adopted were all trained in the English common law tradition. As stated in contemporary sources: "the common law of England is the law of each state, so far as each state has adopted it" (Kurland, Vol. 4, p. 262, No. 40, *U.S. v. Worrall* [1798]. P. 284, No. 48, St. George Tucker [1803]).

At the time, the law of England consisted of two systems existing side by side. In a shorthand description, "common law" (in which the facts are determined by a jury) and "equity law" (in which the facts are determined by the judge). A quote will show what "equity" was understood to mean in this context:

> since in laws all cases cannot be foreseen, or expressed, it is necessary, that when the decrees of the law cannot be applied to particular cases, there should some where [sic] be a power vested of defining those circumstances, which had they been foreseen the legislator would have expressed [Kurland, Vol. 4, p. 235, No. 19, Brutus (1788)].

So the judges had the power to do justice in cases not foreseen by the law.

By providing that federal judicial power extends to "all cases in law and equity arising under this Constitution" (Article III, Section 2), the

Founders recognized this background, which was familiar to every lawyer in what used to be a part of British North America and had now become the United States of America.

Some common law rights, which the Founders deemed of the greatest importance, were expressly stated in the Constitution and in the early amendments. Among these are the right to trial by jury in criminal cases (Article III, Section 2, Clause 3, and Sixth Amendment) and the right to trial by jury in civil cases (Seventh Amendment).

After the Constitution had been adopted, the legal methods of the common law were applied to the Constitution and to the laws made by Congress pursuant to the Constitution.

The theory of the common law was that "it is the duty of the judges to declare, and not to make the law" (Kurland, Vol. 4, p. 263, No. 42, *Fowler v. Lindsay* [1799]).

But, while Congress can make laws at any time, the judges can "declare" the law only when they are asked to do so in a case. And while an act of Congress binds all persons subject to it, a decision of a court, the "law of the case," binds only the parties to the suit. The judicial power

> is capable of acting only when the subject is submitted to it by a party who asserts his rights in the form prescribed by law. It then becomes a case, and the constitution declares, that the judicial power shall extend to all cases arising under the constitution, laws, and treaties of the United States [Kurland, Vol. 4, p. 343, No. 79, *Osborn v. Bank of the United States* (1824)].

There are constitutional questions which are beyond the reach of the courts. The Constitution

> does not extend the judicial power to every violation of the constitution which may possibly take place, but to "a case in law or equity," in which a right, under such law, is asserted in a Court of justice. If the question cannot be brought into a Court, then there is no case in law or equity , and no jurisdiction is given by the words of [Article III] [Kurland, Vol. 4, p.333, No. 74, *Cohens v. Virginia* (1821)].

It was recognized from the beginning that the judges would have to draw on accepted principles of the common law tradition for interpreting the constitution. "The judicial authority consists in applying, according to the principles of right and justice, the constitution and laws to facts and transactions in cases, in which the manner or principles of this application are disputed by the parties interested in them" (Kurland, Vol. 4, p.162, No. 15, Wilson, *Lectures on Law* [1791]).

Where could the judges find the "principles of right and justice" for applying the Constitution to the facts of a given case? By referring to the principles applied in previously decided cases, which in the tradition of the English common law had been collected in written (and printed) reports. The practice of reporting decisions in prior cases was continued in the United States. From the preface to the first printed reports of the decisions of the Supreme Court:

> In a government which is emphatically stiled [sic] a government of laws, the least possible range ought to be left for the discretion of the judge. Whatever tends to render the law certain, equally tends to limit that discretion; and perhaps nothing conduces more to that object than the publication of reports. Every case decided is a check upon the judge. He can not decide a similar case differently, without strong reasons, which, for his own justification, he will wish to make public. The avenues to corruption are thus obstructed, and the sources of litigation closed [Kurland, Vol. 4, p.188, No. 28, William Cranch, Preface (1804)].

Similar cases should be decided in a similar way, that is the basic rule of the common law tradition, which is applied to this day. The judges are to declare which of the preceding cases is most similar to the case at hand.

In *Minnesota v. Carter* (1998) 525 US 83, 142 L Ed 2d 373, 119 S Ct 469, the question was whether a person who had visited another person's apartment for a few hours to help the renter pack cocaine into small bags had the right to claim for himself the protection of the Fourth Amendment against unreasonable searches of the renter's home. Precedent cases had held that based on longstanding social custom an overnight guest in somebody else's home could claim the "right of the people to be *secure in their ... houses ...* against unreasonable searches ..." (Fourth Amendment), while casual visitors were not entitled to this right.

The opinion for the majority of the Court in *Minnesota v. Carter* stated:

> If we regard the overnight guest ... as typifying those who may claim the protection of the Fourth Amendment in the home of another, and one merely "legitimately on the premises" as typifying those who may not do so, the present case is obviously somewhere in between. But

> the purely commercial nature of the transaction engaged in here [bagging cocaine for sale], the relatively short period of time on the premises, and the lack of any previous connection between the [visitor] and the [renter], all lead us to conclude that the [visitor's] situation is closer to that of one simply permitted on the premises. We therefore hold that any search which may have occurred did not violate their Fourth Amendment rights [142 L Ed 2d at p. 381].

Precedent and the rule of deciding similar cases in a similar way here served their purpose as a check on the discretion of the Court. The majority followed the rule when they declared that the case of the cocaine bagger was more similar to the casual visitor precedent than to the overnight guest precedent.

But three justices dissented. They wanted to broaden the scope of the Fourth Amendment.

The precedent cases had reasoned that by accepting an overnight invitation, the guest had made the other person's home to be like his own home, a safe place to stay for the night. This reasoning still had some connection to the constitutional text, "*their* persons, *houses*" (emphasis added).

The dissenting justices picked the word "guest" from its context in the precedent case (by disregarding the qualifier "overnight") and argued that since a "guest" is anybody who has been invited in, once invited in, the premises should become his or her "house" no matter how short the stay or whatever the purpose. Such a result would, in effect, have amended the Fourth Amendment to read: The right of the people to be secure in their persons, their houses, *and any houses in which they may be on the invitation of the owner*, their papers and effects....

Thus the dissenters would have made brand new law. Judges have, from time to time, made new law. Thomas Jefferson, in 1821 in his autobiography, had this comment about the federal judges of his time: "We have seen, too, that contrary to all correct example, they are in the habit of going out of the question before them, to throw an anchor ahead, and grapple further hold for future advances of power" (*The Life and Selected Writings of Thomas Jefferson*, New York: Modern Library, 1944, p. 84).

The dissenting justices in *Minnesota v. Carter* wanted to use the word "guest" as such an anchor thrown ahead to gain further hold for future extension of the Supreme Court's power to supervise police searches and seizures.

Since a "guest" can be generally described as "a person in the house with the owner's consent," the "logic" by which a short term "guest" could claim Fourth Amendment protection could, in the next case down the line, be claimed to apply equally to "any person in the house with the owner's consent." And in the case after that, express consent could be expanded to implied consent, and so on. Thus a chain of analogies could lead, by its "logic," far away from the text of the Constitution.

That the judges must choose between the opposing reasons urged by the parties has been recognized since the early days of the Republic:

> The rule of law is to make such an exposition of the section or clause under consideration, as will comport with its plain meaning when the words are taken in their common and usual acceptation, agreeably to the English language. If the clause is composed of dubious and uncertain expressions, that will admit of different meanings, or if several parts of the instrument [document] seem to contradict, or be repugnant to each other, then the rule is, to make such a construction, if possible, as will be consistent with reason, and agreeable to the intention and purview of the whole instrument [document] taken together [Kurland, Vol. 4, p. 173, No. 21, Senate debate on the Judiciary System (1802)].

Choosing between different and even mutually repugnant meanings of legal texts is not merely "to declare" what the law is. Whenever there are choices, there could be different "laws." By choosing one meaning and excluding other meanings of a given legal text, the judges shape the law for the present case, as well as for the future. The judges start with a legal text, such as a constitutional provision, a statute, or a written decision in a precedent case. They do not "make" that text, but by choosing one of its possible meanings to the exclusion of others, they may "make" a new legal text, which in a future case, may provide a new meaning which you could not find in the original text. In the case of the cocaine bagger the majority refused to amend the Fourth Amendment to cover any and all "guests" in a "house." The dissenters would have liked to make law by extending "overnight guest" to "guest in general" and thereby judicially amend the Fourth Amendment.

That the judges could thus make laws was not generally recognized by the legal profession until the early part of this century, when the so-called "legal realist" scholars analyzed and documented that fact. (For more information see Karl Llewellyn, *The Common Law Tradition, Deciding Appeals*, Boston, Toronto: Little, Brown, 1960.)

But the fact that sometimes there needs to be judge-made law (see Archibald Cox, *The Court and the Constitution*, Boston: Houghton Mifflin, 1987, p. 332) does not mean that the judges should be free to "make" new law all the time, as the judicial activists seem to assume.

We have seen Congress expand its powers, relying on the Commerce Clause and the Spending Clause (see Chapter I). The Supreme Court's power has grown similarly, based on two generally worded clauses of the Constitution, the Due Process of Law Clause (found in the Fifth and the Fourteenth Amendment) and the Equal Protection of the Law Clause (Fourteenth Amendment). But the Court's power expanded and receded twice before the present stage was reached.

The first time was in the *Dred Scott* case, which was overruled by the nation after the Civil War, through the Fourteenth Amendment. The second time occurred in *Lochner v. New York* (1905) 198 US 45, 49 L Ed 937, 25 S Ct 539, and a line of cases following it in which the Supreme Court had struck down economic regulation both by the states and the United States in the name of so-called "liberty of contract," which it held to be guaranteed by the Due Process of Law Clause. These cases were overruled by the Court itself at the time of the "New Deal Amendments." (See Cox, p. 129–144; William H. Rehnquist, *The Supreme Court How It Was, How It Is*, New York: William Morrow, 1987, p. 205–214.) The modern expansion of the judicial power gained momentum in the mid–1950s and crested in the 1970s (Cox, p. 357).

It is not the purpose of this book to give a complete history of that development, but only to highlight some of the areas where the judicial power has gone to the edge of, and finally beyond reasonable interpretation of the Constitution, to the point of amending the Constitution.

The school desegregation case *Brown v. Board of Education of Topeka* (1954) 347 US 483, 98 L Ed 873, 74 S Ct 686, is generally said to mark the beginning of the new era of "judicial activism." *Brown* held that "separate educational facilities are inherently unequal" because "the policy of separating the races is usually interpreted as denoting the inferiority of the negro group" and that therefore state laws requiring racial segregation denied "the equal protection of the laws" (Fourteenth Amendment, Section 1) to the black children who were excluded from the schools of the white majority. This holding, although the Court did not expressly so state, was in essence a return to the Court's original interpretation of Section 1 of the Fourteenth Amendment, exemplified by *Strauder v. West Virginia* (1880) 100 US 303, at p. 307–308, 25 L Ed 664, where the Court had said:

> [The Fourteenth Amendment] ordains that no state shall deprive any person of life, liberty, or property, without due process of law, or deny to any person within its jurisdiction the equal protection of the laws. *What is this but declaring that the law in the States shall be the same for the black as for the white;* that all persons, whether colored or white, shall stand equal before the laws of the States, and, in regard to the colored race, for whose protection the amendment was primarily designed, that no discrimination shall be made against them by law because of their color? The words of the amendment, it is true, are prohibitory, but they contain a necessary implication of a positive immunity, or right, most valuable to the colored race—the right to exemption from unfriendly legislation against them distinctively as colored—exemption from legal discriminations, *implying inferiority in civil society*, lessening the security of their enjoyment of the rights which others enjoy, and discriminations which are steps towards reducing them to the condition of a subject race [emphasis added].

The Court had abandoned this original and true reading of Section 1 of the Fourteenth Amendment in *Plessy v. Ferguson* (1896) 163 US 537, 41 L Ed 256, 16 S Ct 1138, where it upheld a Louisiana law which provided for "separate but equal" accommodations on railroads for blacks and whites. Justice John Marshall Harlan (b.1833–d.1911) dissented vigorously in *Plessy*:

> in view of the constitution, in the eye of the law, there is in this country no superior, dominant, ruling class of citizens. There is no caste here. Our constitution is color-blind, and neither knows nor tolerates classes among citizens. In respect of civil rights, all citizens are equal before the law… In my opinion, the judgment this day rendered will, in time, prove to be quite as pernicious as the decision made by this tribunal in the Dred Scott case [163 U.S. at p. 559].

This proved all too true. The whole system of legally enforced segregation was built on the *Plessy* case.

In the 1954 *Brown* case the Court corrected its, by then, 58-year-old "separate but equal" mistake. The new era of "judicial activism" really began one year later, in the second *Brown* decision (*Brown v. Board of Education of Topeka* [1955] 349 US 294, 75 S Ct 753, 99 L Ed 1083). Here the Supreme Court entered new territory.

Section 5 of the Fourteenth Amendment had given to Congress

the power to enforce Sections 1 through 4 of the Fourteenth Amendment by appropriate legislation. Once the Court had corrected its mistaken "separate but equal" interpretation by the 1954 *Brown* case, it would then have been Congress' turn to enact legislation to abolish segregated schools. However, the Court did not wait for Congress to act, and in 1955 ordered the lower federal courts to use their equity powers to bring about an end to state imposed segregation in schools. These powers were to be used to enforce the rights of the few individuals who had been the named plaintiffs in the *Brown* case and related cases. But in reality the courts now began to deal with millions of children in thousands of schools.

The judicial power traditionally had acted only on the limited number of individuals who are named parties to the suit. But there had been one exception. Where persons so numerous as to make it impracticable to bring them all before the court had a common interest (for example a joint interest in some property), which could be adequately pursued by one or more of such persons acting for the whole class, there the courts under their equity power had permitted suits brought by representatives of the class without insisting that all interested persons must appear before the court.

This traditional type of action fit the circumstances created by the *Brown* decision. In a given school district there would be dozens, hundreds, even thousands of children, all with the common interest of attending desegregated schools. Thus the scope of the judicial power broadened beyond what it had been in the past, and the courts became, in effect, local legislators in the field of education. The courts undertook to do what the Constitution expressly had delegated to Congress by Section 5 of the Fourteenth Amendment. In part this happened because Congress had not immediately enacted enforcement legislation. But the Court did not even wait one year for Congress to act.

Whether enforced by the courts or by Congress, the Equal Protection of the Laws Clause (Fourteenth Amendment, Section 1) achieved in the desegregation cases precisely the purposes for which it had been enacted right after the Civil War, namely that the laws should be the same for blacks and whites. In the next great equal protection case, however, the Court went beyond the historical purposes of the Fourteenth Amendment.

In *Reynolds v. Sims* (1964) 377 US 533, 84 S Ct 1362, 12 L Ed 2d

506, the Court held that the Equal Protection of the Laws Clause (Fourteenth Amendment, Section 1)

> requires that the seats in both houses of a bicameral state legislature must be apportioned on a population basis. Simply stated, an individual's right to vote for state legislators is unconstitutionally impaired when its weight is in a substantial fashion diluted when compared with votes of citizens living in other parts of the State [12 L Ed 2d, at p. 531].

To reach this result the Court relied on great documents of American history: "The conception of political equality from the Declaration of Independence, to Lincoln's Gettysburg Address, to the Fifteenth, Seventeenth and Nineteenth Amendments can mean only one thing—one person, one vote" (12 L Ed 2d, at p. 525).

One person, one vote, certainly fits logically with the term "equal protection of the laws," taken by itself. One is "equal" to one. But as the dissent of Justice John Marshall Harlan (b. 1899–d.1971; grandson of the earlier Justice Harlan) pointed out, to reach this result the Court had to ignore Section 2 of the Fourteenth Amendment:

> The Court relies exclusively on that portion of [Section 1 of] the Fourteenth Amendment which provides that no State shall "deny to any person within its jurisdiction the equal protection of the laws," and disregards entirely the significance of [Section] 2, which reads:
> Representatives shall be apportioned among the several States according to their respective numbers counting the whole number of persons in each State, excluding Indians not taxed. *But when the right to vote at any election for* the choice of electors for President and Vice President of the United States, Representatives in Congress, *the executive and Judicial officers of a State, or the members of the Legislature thereof, is denied* to any of the male inhabitants of such State, being twenty-one years of age, and citizens of the United States, *or in any way abridged*, except for participation in rebellion, or other crime, the basis of representation therein shall be reduced in the proportion which the number of such male citizens shall bear to the whole number of male citizens twenty-one years of age in such State" [emphasis added].
> The Amendment is a single text. It was introduced and discussed as such in the Reconstruction Committee, which reported it to the Congress. It was discussed as a unit in Congress and proposed as a unit to the States, which ratified it as a unit [*Reynolds v. Sims*, 12 L Ed 2d, at p. 545–546].

At the time the Constitution was adopted in 1789, the states retained the power to determine who was entitled to vote in the states' elections. In many states in those days you had to be male, at least 21 years old, able to read and write, and own a certain amount of property. Women had no vote. The new Constitution of the United States limited this power of the states only in one respect: "the Electors [voters] in each State shall have the qualifications requisite for Electors [voters] of the most numerous Branch of the State Legislature" (U.S. Constitution, Article I, Section 2).

So the States could restrict qualifications for voting for congressmen as much as for state assemblymen, but no more.

The words of Section 2 of the Fourteenth Amendment, "But when the right to vote ... is denied to any of the male inhabitants of such State" show that the power of the states to control who votes continued to exist after the adoption of the Fourteenth Amendment in 1868. A State could still lawfully deny the right to vote to blacks. But if it did so, then under Section 2 it would lose as many congressmen as would correspond to the number of blacks whose votes had been denied.

As Justice Harlan pointed out, Section 2 would have been completely unnecessary if "equal protection of the laws" meant equal voting rights. The Fifteenth Amendment, giving the right to vote to blacks in 1870; the Nineteenth Amendment, giving the right to vote to women in 1920; and the Twenty-fourth Amendment, assuring in 1964 every citizen the right to vote regardless of whether they had paid their taxes, would also have been unnecessary.

So the Court's decision to ignore Section 2 and to apply "equal protection" to the number of voters in a voting district, in the words of Justice Harlan "amounts to nothing less than an exercise of the amending power [of the Constitution] by this Court" (*Reynolds v. Sims* [1964] 12 L Ed 2d 506, at p. 545). *Reynolds v. Sims* and the related reapportionment cases are a judicial amendment to the Constitution. We may call it the "Reapportionment Amendment." Like the New Deal Amendment, the Reapportionment Amendment was desired by and has been accepted by the majority of the citizens. One person, one vote, has become part of the Constitution for most elections.

But we should clearly keep in mind that it was a judicial amendment, not a fair reading of the then-existing text of the Fourteenth Amendment. Section 2 of the text had to be ignored in determining whether "equal protection of the laws" was intended to create equal voting rights.

Besides the Reapportionment Amendment, however, the Court has not used the Equal Protection of the Laws Clause to create new constitutional rights. To the contrary, in *San Antonio Independent School District v. Rodriguez* (1973) 411 US 1, 36 L Ed 2d 16, 93 S Ct 2293, the Court declined the invitation to create a federal constitutional right for school children to require the state where the children live to assure that every school district has available and spends the same amount of money per child as every other school district in that state.

The Court said: "It is not the province of this Court to create substantive constitutional rights in the name of guaranteeing equal protection of the laws" (36 L Ed 2d, at p. 43). The Court has adhered to its views in the *San Antonio* case. (See *Vacco v. Quill* (1997) 521 US 793, at p.799, 138 L Ed 2d 834, 117 S Ct 2293.)

But the Court continues to stand ready to create substantive constitutional rights under the Due Process of Law Clause (Fifth and Fourteenth Amendments).

"Due process of law" in plain English means that the judges, when hearing a case, must follow the procedures provided by the Constitution and the laws. The word "process" refers to rules of court procedure, such as trial by jury, confronting and cross-examining witnesses, and assistance of counsel. Juxtaposed to this "procedural law" are the rules of law which give you the rights which you may assert in court, such as the right to be paid for your labor, the right to vote, the right to marry, and the right to inherit property. These are called "substantive law." To be able to say that a substantive rule of law violates the "due process of law" clause, the courts had to disregard the word "process" which limits the clause to procedural rules. To totally disregard the word "process" is the same as to strike it out. So the "due process of law" clause of the Fourteenth Amendment effectively reads today: "nor shall any state deprive any person of life, liberty, or property without due _____ law..." And the judges say what law is "due."

This is called "substantive due process." One justice has called this an oxymoron, since it translates into "substantive procedure" (*United States v. Carlton* (1994) 512 US 26, 129 L Ed 2d 22, at p.33, 114 S Ct 2018).

What the Court has found to be "due law," over the years amounts to a judge-made "Bill of Individual Liberties," which the Court described a few years ago in these words:

[The] Due Process Clause protects individual liberty against "certain government actions regardless of the fairness of the procedures used to implement them"...

...In a long line of cases, we have held that, in addition to the specific freedoms protected by the Bill of Rights, the "liberty" specially protected by the Due Process Clause, includes the rights to marry ... to have children ... to direct the education and the upbringing of one's children ... to maintain marital privacy ... to use contraception ... to bodily integrity ... and to abortion. We have also assumed, that the Due Process Clause protects the traditional right to refuse unwanted life—saving medical treatment [*Washington v. Glucksberg* (1997) 521 US 702, 138 L Ed 2d 772, at p.787, 117 S Ct 2258].

Three points should be kept in mind.

First, the judicial amendment striking the limiting word "process" is not recent. It has occurred from time to time since the *Dred Scott* case in 1857 where the Court said:

an act of Congress which deprives a citizen of the United States of his ... property [slaves], merely because he ... brought his property [slaves] into a particular territory of the United States ... could hardly be dignified with the name of due process of law [*Dred Scott v. Sanford* (1857) 60 US (19 How.) 393, at p.450, 15 L Ed 691].

The act of Congress in question, known as the Missouri Compromise, prohibited slavery in territories of the United States north of 36 degrees, 30 minutes northern latitude. The act was not procedural but substantive law in these territories. To be able to say that Congress under the Due Process of Law Clause had no power to make such a substantive law, the Court had to ignore the limiting word "process."

Secondly, the concept that courts have an inherent power, even without the Due Process of Law Clause, to protect the people against legislative acts that violate fundamental principles dates back to the early years of the Republic and beyond. For example, in *Calder v. Bull* (1798) 3 Dall. 386 (Kurland, Vol. 3, p. 402–403, No. 10) the court said:

I cannot subscribe to the omnipotence of a state legislature, or that it is absolute and without control; although its authority should not be expressly restrained by the constitution ... of the state.... There are certain vital principles in our free republican government, which will determine and overrule an apparent and flagrant abuse of legislative power; as to ... take away the security for personal liberty, or private property, for the protection whereof the government was established.

Today this traditional power of the courts is asserted under the label "substantive due process," and is an expression of the belief that the courts must have the power to protect individuals against arbitrary government action.

Thirdly, the courts have made mistakes in using this power. The *Dred Scott* case led to the Civil War and the *Lochner* case led to continued social strife. *Roe v. Wade* keeps the nation divided and citizens continue to kill fellow citizens over the issue.

It is noteworthy that in each of the three big mistake cases, there were dissenting opinions which pointed out that the Court was legislating, instead of merely interpreting the Constitution. (*Dred Scott v. Sanford* (1857) 60 US [19 How.] 393, at p. 620–621; *Lochner v. New York* (1905) 198 US 45, at p.65 and p.74, 49 L Ed 937, 25 S Ct 539; *Roe v. Wade* (1973) 410 US 113, 35 L Ed 2d 147, at p. 195–198, 93 S Ct 705.)

But apart from these mistakes the Court's Bill of Individual Liberties has been accepted by a great majority of the citizens.

There is currently a struggle within the Court about the standards which should be used in adding new rights to this Bill of Individual Liberties. Some justices are trying to limit the Court to adopting only those previously undeclared rights which can be found in "our nation's history, legal traditions, and practices.... For these rights ... the primary and most reliable indication of [a national] consensus is ... the pattern of enacted laws (*Washington v. Glucksberg* 521 US 702, 138 L Ed 2d 772, at p. 781, 117 S Ct 2258).

This approach would provide somewhat objective standards, that would help to defeat demand for new "due law" constitutional rights that come before the Court as "nothing more than [a] bald assertio[n]" without "any historical, textual, or controlling precedential support." Under such somewhat objective standards the Court would "decline to fashion a new due process right out of thin air."(*County of Sacramento v. Lewis* (1998) 523 US 833, 140 L Ed 2d 1043, at p. 1067, 118 S Ct 1708).

But another, more subjective approach was used in *County of Sacramento v. Lewis*. In that case a police officer had followed a speeding motorcycle with two persons on it. The chase reached speeds up to 100 mph. The motorcyclist tried a sharp left turn during which the backseat rider of the cycle was thrown into the path of the police car which was unable to stop in time. The suit alleged the deprivation of a "substantive due process right to life." The opinion for the majority of the

Court stated: "So-called 'substantive due process' prevents the government from engaging in conduct that 'shocks the conscience'" (140 L Ed 2d, at p. 1058). The Court concluded that the conduct of the police officer did not "shock the conscience." An accident happened while the officer was doing his duty.

Two justices criticized the use of the "shocks the conscience" test. They pointed out that better guidance could be found in the nation's history. Historically the guarantee of due process has been applied to *deliberate* decisions of government officials to deprive a person of life, liberty or property, not to accidents. It is a matter of state law whether the police should or should not conduct high speed pursuits. In legislation allocating the risks and benefits to society of such pursuits "the people ... and their elected representatives may vote their conscience. But for judges to overrule that democratically adopted policy judgment on the ground that it shocks *their* consciences is not judicial review but judicial governance" (140 L Ed 2d, at p. 1069).

This is where the Due Law Clause stands today. Under either of these standards the Court may "recognize" federal constitutional rights that nobody previously heard about, and add them to the Bill of Individual Liberties.

Historically, most of such incremental amendments to the Constitution have been accepted by the majority of the citizens, and we are grateful for the gradual increase of "ordered liberty" these judicial amendments have brought about. But, as we have seen, the Court has made occasional mistakes, and it is the purpose of this book to show how a majority of the citizens could correct such a mistake without having to use the drastic and inappropriate remedy of impeachment for an honest error, or use the exceedingly time consuming and major surgery of a constitutional amendment to counter small incremental judicial amendments.

We are dealing here with a shortcoming in the design of the Constitution, which was recognized as such before the Constitution had even been adopted.

In 1788, a publicist using the pen name "Brutus" analyzing the proposed Constitution said:

> the judicial [judiciary] under this system have power which is above the legislative, and which indeed transcends any power before given to a judicial [judiciary] by any free government under heaven...

> ... There is no power above them, to controul [sic] any of their decisions. There is no authority that can remove them, and they cannot be controuled [sic] by the laws of the legislature. In short, they are independent of the people, of the legislature, and of every power under heaven. Men placed in this situation will generally soon feel themselves independent of heaven itself...
>
> ... The supreme cort [sic] ... have a right, independent of the legislature, to give a construction to the constitution and every part of it, and there is no power provided in this system to correct their construction or do it away [Kurland, Vol. 4, p. 239, No. 22, Brutus (1788)].

But it was also recognized that the Constitution could not work without an independent judiciary:

> an act of parliament [of Great Britain], combining, as it does, the will of the crown, and of the legislature, is absolute and omnipotent. It cannot lawfully be resisted, or disobeyed. The judiciary is bound to carry it into effect at every hazard, even though it should subvert private rights and public liberty. But it is far otherwise in a republic, like our own, with a limited constitution, prescribing at once the powers of the rulers, and the rights of the citizens. This very circumstance would seem conclusively to show, that the independence of the judiciary is absolutely indispensable to preserve the balance of such a constitution. In no other way can there be any practical restraint upon the acts of the government, or any practical enforcement of the rights of the citizens [Kurland, Vol. 4, p. 205, No. 38, Story, *Commentaries on the Constitution* (1833); see also: p. 184, No. 26, St. George Tucker, *Blackstone's Commentaries* (1803)].

How can we control an erroneous interpretation of the Constitution by the Supreme Court without affecting this indispensable independence? The control must not operate on the persons of the Supreme Court justices. Removal or personal censure would destroy their independence. Impeachment for an honest error is out of the question. To amend the Constitution in every such case is not practicable. The point where control may be exercised is the erroneous decision itself. But the decision between the parties, known as the law of the case, must not be changed. It is of the essence of our judicial system that a final judgment of a court of last resort is indeed final as between the parties. So the control must operate by limiting the effect of the decision as precedent in future cases.

Chapter III

Education

Congress has informally amended the Fourteenth Amendment to the Constitution by requiring the states to provide "equal opportunity" to their citizens, instead of "equal protection of the laws."

From the early days of the Republic, Congress has supported education. This grew naturally out of Congress' power "to dispose of and make all needful Rules and Regulations respecting the Territory ... belonging to the United States" (Article IV, Section 3, Clause 2 of the U.S. Constitution).

When public land was opened for settlement, some part of it was reserved for schools. As early as 1792, Congress authorized the President to grant to a real estate developer "in trust for the purpose of establishing an academy and other public schools and seminaries of learning, one complete township" (*United States Statutes at Large*, Vol. 1, at p. 267).

A "township" is a standard unit of the U.S. Government Survey, containing approximately 36 square miles in 36 square sections which are numbered in such sequence that sections 16, 15, 21, and 22 surround the center of the township. One of the centrally located sections was typically reserved for school purposes in most acts of Congress authorizing the sale of surveyed public lands to settlers.

An act of Congress of March 3, 1803, authorized the sale of certain public lands in the Mississippi Territory

> with the exception of the section number sixteen, which shall be reserved in each township for the support of schools within the same, with the exception also of thirty six sections [one township] to be located in one body by the Secretary of the Treasury for the use of Jefferson College [United States Statutes at Large, Vol. 2, at p. 234].

This pattern of school support was followed for more than a decade.

(See *United States Statutes at Large*, Vol. 2, at p. 279 [1804]; Vol. 2, at p. 382–383 [1806]; Vol. 2, at p. 480 [1808]; Vol. 3, at p. 163 [1815]; Vol. 3, at p. 309 [1816]; Vol. 3, at p. 319 [1816].)

After states had been formed in the territories, Congress authorized the new states to sell the school land and create endowments from the proceeds to support education. The act of Congress of February 15, 1843 is typical for this approach:

> The legislatures of Illinois, Arkansas, Louisiana and Tennessee, be, and they are hereby authorized to provide by law for the sale and conveyance in fee simple, of all or any part of the lands heretofore reserved and appropriated by Congress for the use of schools within said States, and to invest the money arising from the sales thereof in some productive fund, the proceeds of which shall be forever applied, under the direction of said Legislatures, to the use and support of schools within the several townships and districts of country for which they were originally reserved and set apart, and for no other purpose whatever [*United States Statutes at Large*, Vol. 5, at p. 600].

By 1862, the endowment approach still persisted, with specific focus on creating agricultural colleges. Public land was donated to the states. The states were authorized to sell this land, provided

> that all moneys derived from the sale of the lands ... by the States ... shall be invested in stocks of the United States, or of the States, or some other safe stocks, yielding not less than five per centum upon the par value of said stocks, and that the moneys so invested shall constitute a perpetual fund, the capital of which shall remain forever undiminished ... and the interest of which shall be inviolably appropriated, by each State which may take and claim the benefit of this act, to the endowment, support and maintenance of at least one college where the leading subject shall be, without excluding other scientific and classical studies, and including military tactics, to teach such branches of learning as are related to agriculture and the mechanic arts, in such manner as the Legislatures of the States may respectively prescribe, in order to promote the liberal and practical education of the industrial classes in the several pursuits and professions in life [*United States Statutes at Large*, Vol. 12, at p. 504 (1862)].

Congress attached a few conditions to these grants to which the states had to agree by enacting legislation: The states had to promise to make good any capital loss of an endowment. None of the money could be used in any way for buildings. Ten percent of the money could be used to buy land for experimental farms. The states had to establish at least one agricultural college within five years and had to make annual reports of the progress of each agricultural college.

Near the end of the century the pattern changed slightly. Instead of granting public lands to the states, money in the U.S. Treasury resulting from the sale of public lands was appropriated to be paid to the states for agricultural colleges, under similar conditions as in 1862 (*United States Statutes at Large*, Vol. 26, p. 417–418 [1890]). Presumably there were no longer sufficient unsold public lands in each state to make, in every state, grants of land rather than money, but the source of the money grants remained the public lands.

Up to this point congressional support for schools was a net addition to the wealth of each state. Public lands of the United States, or money realized from the sale of such land, did not come out of the pockets of the citizens.

The power of Congress to dispose of public lands in this manner was felt to be clearly given by the terms under which the original public lands had been ceded by the states to the United States and by the power to dispose of them found in Article IV, Section 3, Clause 2 of the Constitution.

As Justice Story put it in 1833,

> the public lands hold out, after the discharge of the national debt, ample revenues to be devoted to the cause of education and sound learning, and to internal improvements, without trenching upon the property, or embarrassing the pursuits of the people by burthensome [sic] taxation. The constitutional objection to the appropriation of the other revenues of the government to such objects has not been supposed to apply to an appropriation of the proceeds of the public lands. The cessions of that territory were expressly made for the common benefit of the United States; and therefore constitute a fund, which may be properly devoted to any objects, which are for the common benefit of the Union [Kurland, Vol. 4, p. 558, No. 8].

Note that at the time Story wrote the dispute about the scope of the "Taxing for the General Welfare Clause" was still continuing, and the powers of Congress were still understood to be limited. As Story put it, Congress has no power "to interfere with the systems of education, the poor laws, or the road laws of the states" (Kurland, Vol. 2, p. 467, No. 28).

In the early years of this century, proceeds from the sale of public lands ceased to be the source of revenue for the federal support of the agricultural colleges. By the act of February 23, 1917, for example, the money appropriated by Congress to help the states pay the salaries of teachers in the agricultural colleges came "out of any money in the Treasury not otherwise appropriated" (*United States Statutes at Large*, Vol. 39, p. 929 [1917]), that is to say out of the general revenue of the United States.

At this point, therefore, Congress' power to dispose of the public lands could no longer serve as the constitutional basis for Congress' involvement in education. But the act of February 23, 1917, did not specify on what part of the Constitution this exercise of congressional power was now based.

At the same time, there was a change in the degree of control exercised over the states with regard to this money. The money could no longer be spent by the states, subject only to a few conditions specified by Congress in the statute itself. Now the Federal Board for Vocational Education was set up to preside over doling out the money. The states that wished to receive federal money had to submit, for approval by the federal board, plans

> showing the kind of vocational education for which it is proposed that the appropriation shall be used; the kinds of schools and equipment; courses of study; methods of instruction; qualifications of teachers; and, in the case of agricultural subjects, the qualifications of supervisors or directors; plans for the training of teachers; and, in the case of agricultural subjects, plans for the supervision of agricultural education, as provided for in Section 10.

Section 10, in turn, specified that the federal money could be used only for salaries of teachers and supervisors, and

> that such education shall be that which is under public supervision or control; that the controlling purpose of such education shall be to fit [prepare] for useful employment; that such education shall be of less than college grade and be designed to meet the needs of persons over fourteen years of age who have entered upon or who are preparing to enter upon the work of the farm or of the farm home; that the State or local community, or both, shall provide the necessary plant and equipment determined upon by the State board, with the approval of the Federal Board for Vocational Education, as the minimum requirement for such education in schools and classes in the State; that the amount expended for the maintenance of such education in any school or class receiving the benefit of such appropriation shall be not less annually than the amount fixed by the State board, with

the approval of the Federal board as the minimum for such schools or classes in the State; that such schools shall provide for directed or supervised practice in agriculture, either on a farm provided for by the school or other farm, for at least six months per year; that the teachers, supervisors, or directors of agricultural subjects shall have at least the minimum qualifications determined for the State by the State board, with the approval of the Federal Board for Vocational Education [*United States Statutes at Large*, Vol. 39, p. 929, at p. 934].

I have quoted in such detail from this statute because it sets the pattern for federal-state "cooperation" that we find today in the congressional legislation concerning education.

Congress draws money from the people of the states, by income, excise, and other taxes. Congress, after taking a cut to pay for the federal education bureaucracy, offers some of this money back to the states on condition that the states "voluntarily" pass laws which follow Congress' instructions as to how the education in question should be conducted.

And the instructions go into detail. In the example of the act of February 23, 1917: The course must go on for at least six months. A minimum amount of money must be spent, the education must not be of college grade, the teachers must have federally approved minimum qualifications, and so forth—or else no federal money. Sure, the state board initially determines how much money should be spent and what qualifications the teachers should have, but the federal board has the last word.

Besides the beginning of federal—state "cooperation," we see here the beginning of the "unfunded mandate." To get the federal money for the salaries, the state or locality must raise the money for "the necessary plant and equipment," and although the state board is asked to determine what is "necessary," ultimately the federal board decides what is "necessary," i.e., how much money the state or locality must raise.

The intentions of Congress in devising this scheme of "cooperating with the States in paying the salaries of teachers, supervisors, and directors of agricultural subjects" (at p. 929) were undoubtedly the best, and the conditions imposed on the states were probably reasonable for achieving the specific purpose of this legislation. But today, some 80 years later, we see that dealing with the states directly and using (and shaping) their administrative organizations has shifted the federal-state balance decisively.

In 1917 the constitutional basis for Congress' involvement in education presumably was the "Taxing for the General Welfare Clause" (nowadays called the "Spending Power"), but Congress did not state this expressly in the act of February 23, 1917.

In more recent times, Congress has relied on other parts of the Constitution. The National Defense Education Act of 1958 relied on Congress' power to provide for the common defense (Article I, Section 8, Clause 1) in furthering education in science, mathematics, modern foreign languages, and technology.

In the Equal Educational Opportunities Act of 1974, Congress relied on the Equal Protection Clause of the Fourteenth Amendment for its involvement with education in the states. The Equal Protection Clause is a part of Section 1 of the Fourteenth Amendment, added to the Constitution after the end of the Civil War. The immediate purpose of the amendment was to give U.S. and State citizenship to the newly freed blacks and protect them against state laws that might try to infringe on these citizenship rights. The words of the Equal Protection Clause are: "nor [shall any State] deny to any person within its jurisdiction the equal protection of the laws."

What is the common sense meaning of these words in today's English? Obviously the words apply to every "person." Every human being is a "person"; that much is clear. Every state has a body of laws that apply to all persons inside the state's boundaries. That must be what the phrase "the laws" refers to. Generally speaking, all people inside the state's boundaries can sue or be sued, or prosecuted, in the courts of that state, so that must be what the phrase "within its jurisdiction" refers to. The laws of a State create rights and duties of persons in the state. "Protection" of the laws comes to people from the enforcement of these rights and duties by the state, or by private lawsuits in the state's courts.

When is protection "equal?" Can you treat all persons living in a state, from day-old babies to aging adults in all ways and at all times "equally?" If every person living in a state every year had to pay a tax of one thousand dollars, every person an equal amount, would that be "equal protection of the laws?" The words of the clause, read literally, seem to say so, but common sense tells us that this could not be intended. The state must be allowed to divide people into different classifications (for example, by the amount of property they own or income they receive), and then treat everybody in the class the same way.

The Equal Protection Clause, read this way, tells the state that it cannot give a particular protection to one person in a class and deny it to another in the same class. If a state has a law making perjury a crime in order to protect the right of a party to a lawsuit to have the case decided according to the true facts, then the state cannot decline to prosecute lying witnesses in cases where a woman is the plaintiff, but prosecute lying witnesses in cases where a man is the plaintiff. Or, if a state has a statute exempting from property taxes land used for a church, it cannot allow the exemption to churches with white congregations, but deny it to churches with black congregations.

On its face, the Equal Protection Clause says nothing about what kinds of laws a state must have. It doesn't say that a state must have laws against perjury or laws giving tax exemptions to church property. What "protection of the laws" a state will provide is left up to its legislature.

But it is reasonably implied in the words "equal protection of the laws," that a state cannot have one statute which gives property tax exemptions to "white churches," and another statute which denies such exemptions to "black churches." In this sense the clause forbids a state not only from applying a given law differently to blacks and whites, to men and women, and so on, but also from making different laws on the same subject for blacks and whites, for men and women, and thereby denying them equal treatment.

This much we can see by looking at the words of the clause. We cannot tell, however, by looking at the words of the clause what "protection" a state must give to the persons in its jurisdiction. It is fair to say that the clause, by the words in which it is expressed, does not create rights to any particular level of protection but only requires that such protection as a state legislature chooses to give must be equally applied to all persons in the state who reasonably are in the same classification.

The Supreme Court has read the Equal Protection Clause in this common sense way: "It is not the province of this Court to create substantive constitutional rights in the name of guaranteeing equal protection of the laws" (*San Antonio Independent School District v. Rodriguez* [1973] 411 U.S. 1, 36 L Ed 2d 16, at p. 43, 93 S Ct 1278).

Or, as expressed by a justice concurring in the majority opinion in the *San Antonio* case:

Unlike other provisions of the Constitution, the Equal Protection Clause confers no substantive rights and creates no substantive liberties. The function of the Equal Protection Clause, rather, is simply to measure the validity of *classifications* created by state laws. There is hardly a law on the books that does not affect some people differently from others. But the basic concern of the Equal Protection Clause is with state legislation whose purpose or effect is to create discrete and objectively identifiable classes. And with respect to such legislation, it has long been settled that the Equal Protection Clause is offended only by laws that are invidiously discriminatory—only by classifications that are wholly arbitrary or capricious [36 L Ed 2d, at p. 58].

Section 5 of the Fourteenth Amendment gives Congress the power to enforce the Equal Protection Clause by "appropriate legislation."

The Equal Educational Opportunities Act of 1974 is claimed to be such enforcement legislation. Especially relevant here are three sections of Title 20 of the *United States Code*:

Section 1701

(a) The Congress declares it to be the policy of the United States that—

(1) all children enrolled in public schools are entitled to equal educational opportunity without regard to race, color, sex, or national origin...

Section 1702

(a) The Congress finds that—

(1) the maintenance of dual school systems in which students are assigned to schools solely on the basis of race, color, sex, or national origin denies to those students the equal protection of the laws guaranteed by the fourteenth amendment....

Section 1703

No state shall deny equal educational opportunity to an individual on account of his or her race, color, sex, or national origin, by—

(a) the deliberate segregation by an educational agency of students on the basis of race, color, or national origin among or within schools;

(b) the failure of an educational agency which has formerly practiced ... deliberate segregation to take affirmative steps ... to remove the vestiges of a dual school system...

(f) the failure by an educational agency *to take appropriate action* to overcome language barriers that impede equal participation by its students in its instructional programs [emphasis added].

In major part, this statute aims at the initial historical purpose of the Equal Protection Clause, i.e., to protect people against discrimination based on race or color. While the words "race" or "color" do not appear in the Fourteenth Amendment they are clearly implied by the historical origin of the amendment. The phrase "national origin" also does not appear in the Fourteenth Amendment, but it is clearly implied from Section 1 of the amendment, "all persons born or *naturalized* in the United States ... are citizens of the United States" (emphasis added).

To include "sex" as a forbidden basis of discrimination, one has to go beyond the words of the Fourteenth Amendment, to the Nineteenth Amendment (adopted in 1920), which prohibits the United States and all the states individually from denying or abridging the right to vote "on account of sex." While the Nineteenth Amendment prohibits only the denial of the right to vote, to extend this to all civic rights is reasonable, even if it is not expressly supported by the words of the Constitution.

The main purpose of the quoted statute is to prohibit segregation. A state denies equal protection of the laws if it classifies children by race. Since the state has decided to provide free public education, it must provide it equally to all children.

Note, however, the subtle shift from prohibiting denial of equal treatment under the education laws a state has chosen to enact, to an "entitlement" of "equal educational opportunity" (Section 1701 [a][1]). This shift becomes concrete in subsection (f), which states a mandate to "overcome language barriers." Traditionally, public education in most of the United States was conducted in the English language. Under this statute, either the English speaking teacher must take extra time to help children who do not understand English, or special teachers must be hired for these children. That means that not only equal resources, but *more* resources must be devoted to these children. Does that still come within the normal meaning of the words "equal protection of the laws?"

It seems that Congress has begun here to tell the states what "protection" they must provide, rather than hold them to applying equally whatever "protection" they had chosen to provide.

In 1979, Congress created the federal Department of Education by the Department of Education Organization Act. For this law Congress apparently relied on the Taxing for the General Welfare Clause (Spending Clause) and the Equal Protection Clause. (Again the sections quoted are from Title 20 of the *United States Code*.)

> Section 3402
>
> The Congress declares that the establishment of a Department of Education is in the public interest, will promote the general welfare of the United States ... therefore the purposes of this chapter are—
>
> (1) to strengthen the Federal commitment to ensuring access to equal educational opportunity for every individual;
>
> (2) to supplement and complement the efforts of States ... to improve the quality of education...
>
> (6) to improve the management and efficiency of Federal education activities, especially with respect to the process, procedures, and administrative structures for the dispersal [sic] of Federal funds, as well as the reduction of unnecessary and duplicative burdens and constraints, including unnecessary paperwork, on the recipients of federal funds...

Note the interesting word, "dispersal" of federal funds, instead of "disbursal." (Disperse: 1. to drive or send off in various directions; scatter. *The Random House Dictionary of the English Language*, Unabridged Edition, 1967.) The word was correct, however, in the 18th century.

So a new bureaucracy was set up to improve the efficiency of the old one, and, whether the quality of education in fact has been improved, after billions of dollars have been "dispersed" for twenty years, I will leave for you to judge.

It is not the purpose of this book to give a complete history of congressional involvement in education in the states, but to highlight the changes in the way Congress has interpreted the Constitution, and the shifting of states' powers to Congress by means of that interpretation.

We turn then to the most recent major congressional enactment in the field of education, the Individuals with Disabilities Education Act (IDEA), as completely revised in 1997. (This is found in Title 20 of the *United States Code*, beginning with Section 1400.)

Section 1400 (c)

The Congress finds the following:

(1) Disability is a natural part of the human experience and in no way diminishes the right of individuals to participate in or contribute to society. Improving educational results for children with disabilities is an essential element of our national policy of ensuring equality of opportunity, full participation, independent living, and economic self-sufficiency for individuals with disabilities....

(6) While States, local educational agencies ... are responsible for providing an education for all children with disabilities, it is in the national interest that the Federal Government have a role in assisting State and local efforts to educate children with disabilities in order to improve results for such children and ensure equal protection of the law.

(7)(A) The Federal Government must be responsive to the growing needs of an increasingly more diverse society. A more equitable allocation of resources is essential for the Federal Government to meet its responsibility to provide an equal educational opportunity for all individuals.

The purpose of this law is undoubtedly worthy. But can congressional power to achieve this purpose fairly be found in the Constitution? Congress states that the federal government should "have a role in assisting" state and local efforts in the education of children with disabilities "in order to improve results for such children and to *ensure equal protection of the law*" (emphasis added). Does this "role" come included in Congress' power "to regulate commerce among the several states," or in Congress' power to tax and "provide for the common defense and general welfare of the United States," or does it derive from Congress' power to enforce the Equal Protection Clause by "appropriate legislation?"

It appears that for IDEA, Congress relied on the Equal Protection Clause for the power it assumes "to improve results ... and to ensure equal protection of the law" (Section 1400 [c][6]). And without stating so expressly, Congress also relied on the Taxing for the General Welfare Clause (Spending Clause), by setting up the typical Spending Power scheme:

Section 1412 (a)

A state is eligible for assistance ... if the State demonstrates to the satisfaction of the Secretary [of Education] that the State has in effect policies and procedures to ensure that it meets each of the following conditions:

(1)(A) A free appropriate public education is available to all children with disabilities residing in the State.... including children with disabilities who have been suspended or expelled from school.

Section 1412 (a) lists 23 conditions. A state which desires its fair share of the federal money must meet each of these 23 conditions—or else no return of that state's taxpayers' money to the state.

Congress imposed these conditions to "ensure equal protection of the law," but of what law? Of the laws the states have enacted, or of the law that Congress is laying down?

A State which desires its fair share of returned taxpayer money must make available "a free appropriate public education" for children with disabilities. The education has to be "appropriate" to the "satisfaction" of the secretary of education. An education is "appropriate" if it is "provided in conformity with the individualized education program required under section 1414(d)..." (Section 1401[8]).

Section 1414 (d) covers three and a half pages in the *United States Code*. It requires school districts to work up a detailed "individualized education program" (IEP) which must contain "a statement of the special education and related services and supplementary aids and services to be provided to the child, or on behalf of the child, and a statement of the program modifications or supports for school personnel that will be provided for the child."

To administer the IEP, an "individualized education program team" (IEP Team) must be formed, consisting of the parent, at least one regular education teacher, at least one special education teacher, a school district representative who is "Qualified to provide ... specially designed instruction to meet the unique needs of children with disabilities," an "individual who can interpret the instructional implications of evaluation results..." and so on, adding up to at least seven persons, including the child himself, when "appropriate."

No doubt this is worthy protection—but is it "equal" protection? So much individualized attention costs considerably more money than does the schooling given to children without disabilities. It is thus, in terms of money, more than equal.

Does a state deny the equal protection of the laws to children, if the state spends exactly the same amount of money per child, regardless of whether the child is rich or poor, smart or dumb, healthy or sickly, disabled or not disabled?

By the plain words of the clause, "equal" would seem to require that no child should receive less money, but would not seem to require more money for one child than for another. Thus a state may not discriminate *against* any child. But does the clause require that the state must discriminate *in favor* of any children?

In the IDEA, Congress has read the clause in the latter way. To put teeth into this reading, Congress has abolished the states' right (given by the Eleventh Amendment) to be sued only with their consent. So now disabled children can sue their state in federal court to give them their federal right to an appropriate free public education by the state. (Title 20 of the *United States Code*, Section 1403.)

The IDEA has been called a model of "cooperative federalism" (*Beth V. v. Carroll* (1996) 87 F 3d 80, at p. 82).

To recapitulate, Congress takes money for stateside education from the citizens of the states. Congress takes a cut of this money to pay for the federal education bureaucracy. Congress then offers some of this money back to the states, if they will agree to raise additional money, to pay for whatever Congress decides is an "appropriate" free public education. If they don't agree, they will not get any of their citizens' money back. Do what Congress tells you if you want some of your money back—equals "cooperative federalism."

It appears that in the IDEA, Congress has gone beyond the plain words of the Equal Protection Clause and, instead of "nor shall [any state] deny to any person within its jurisdiction the equal protection of the laws," it is now equivalent to: nor shall any state deny to any individual within its jurisdiction equal opportunities.

"Protection" means "1. the act of protecting; state of being protected; preservation from injury or harm." "Opportunity" means "1. an appropriate or favorable time or occasion; 2. a situation or condition favorable for attainment of a goal; 3. a good position, change or prospect for advancement" (*The Random House Dictionary of the English Language*, Unabridged Edition, 1967). These two words have different meanings. When you substitute the one for the other, you change the meaning of the Equal Protection Clause, you amend it to become the Equal Opportunity Clause.

Since Congress has power to enforce the clause by appropriate legislation, it will now be Congress who determines when opportunities are equal for all individuals living in a state, and in what cases the state must provide extra money to persons in a given classification, *to each according to his need*, to give them equal opportunities with others in the same classification.

The aim of giving the rich and the poor, the able and the disabled, the same opportunity is worthy, but it is a great step beyond the plain words "equal protection of the laws." Congress has, in effect, amended the Equal Protection Clause and drastically changed the balance of powers between the federal government and the states.

It may be argued that Congress, in any event, has the power to impose the conditions of the IDEA under the Taxing for the General Welfare Clause (Spending Clause). As we have seen (Chapter I), the Supreme Court said in *South Dakota v. Dole* (the drinking age case) that Congress may achieve indirectly by conditions to federal grants what Congress lacks power to legislate directly, so long as the exercise of the Spending Power is for "the general welfare."

As "Brutus" pointed out in 1788 (Chapter I), the Taxing for the General Welfare Clause may be read so as to "authorize Congress to do any thing which in their judgment will tend to provide for the general welfare, and this amounts to the same thing as general and unlimited powers of legislation in all cases" (Kurland, Vol. 4, p. 237, No. 20).

Should we accept these readings of the clause? What does "general welfare of the United States" mean in today's English?

From the context in which the phrase occurs, "The Congress shall have Power to lay and collect Taxes ... to pay the Debts and provide for the common Defence and general welfare of the United States" (Article I, Section 8, Clause 1), one could conclude that the "Welfare" referred to is "general" in the same sense as the "Defence" is "common" The "common Defence" is the defense of all of the states comprising the United States taken together, and of all of the citizens in all states, not the defense of any given state, region, or population group, taken separately. By the same token, the "general Welfare" would be the welfare of all of the citizens in all of the states taken together, and not the welfare of particular groups or classes of Americans.

This is the way the clause was understood during the 19th century by Thomas Jefferson, James Madison and their Republican party; by Andrew Jackson, Martin Van Buren; and their Democratic Republican party, and others. For a few examples:

• In 1876 President Grant objected to Congress about money appropriated for harbor and river improvements that were "works of purely private or local interest, in no sense national" (as quoted in *Clinton v. City of New York* [1998] 524 US 417, 141 L Ed 2d 393, at p. 432, 118 S Ct 2091).

• In 1854, President Franklin Pierce vetoed a bill, which would have granted to the states ten million acres of public land to be sold, proceeds invested, and the interest "to be appropriated to the maintenance of the indigent insane within the several states."

In his veto message President Pierce said about the Taxing for the General Welfare Clause (Article I, Section 8, Clause 1):

> I take the received and just construction of that article, as if written to lay and collect taxes, duties, imposts, and excises *in order* to pay the debts and *in order* to provide for the common defense and general welfare. It is not a substantive general power to provide for the welfare of the United States, but is a limitation on the grant of power to raise money by taxes, duties and imposts. If it were otherwise, all the rest of the Constitution, consisting of carefully enumerated and cautiously guarded grants of specific powers, would have been useless, if not delusive [as quoted in *Steward Machine Co. v. Davis* (1937) 301 US 548, at p. 605, 81 L Ed 1279, 57 S Ct 883].

• In 1833, President Andrew Jackson criticized the "log rolling system of Internal Improvements, Squandering the taxes raised on the whole people, in benefiting particular classes and maintaining a personal influence by partial legislation in congress." This was a constant concern of President Jackson. In the context of legislation providing for distribution of the budget surplus to the States,

> it profoundly disturbed him that he should be the President to begin a practice that would end with the government giving money to states, individuals, and corporations and then prescribing the rules by which they must behave [Robert V. Remini, *Andrew Jackson*, History Book Club, New York, 1998, Vol. 3, at pp. 92, 326, respectively].

• In 1831, James Madison gave a vivid example of the difference between national and local:

> What again of the interval between clearing of its sawyers etc. the Mississippi the commercial highway for half the nation, and removing obstructions by which the navigation of an inconsiderable stream may be extended a few miles only within a single state [Kurland,

Vol. 3, p. 262, No. 19. A "sawyer" is a tree swept away by the river, which is bobbing up and down, *Oxford English Dictionary*, Compact Edition, 1971].

• In 1817, Thomas Jefferson, writing approvingly of President Madison's veto of an "act for internal improvements," pointed out the evil of purely local improvement legislation.

> intrigue, negotiation, and the barter of votes might become as habitual in Congress, as they are in those legislatures which have the appointment of officials, and which, with us, is called "logging," the term of the farmers for their exchanges of aid in rolling together the logs of their newly cleared grounds [Kurland, Vol. 2, p. 452, No. 25].

By this traditional reading of "general Welfare," building interstate highways might be for the "general" welfare because every American could use them in traveling by car or by bus. But urban redevelopment in Chicago or Detroit would not be for the "general" welfare, it would be for the welfare of Chicago or Detroit.

To make urban redevelopment "national" you would need the old saw "What's good for _____ is good for the country" for support.

But if we take general welfare from the context of "common Defence and general Welfare," we can arrive at an unlimited meaning. It can be argued that any good deed done to or for any individual, by any individual or by the government, adds to the sum of goodness in the country and thus adds to the "general Welfare." In that sense, a levee on the Humboldt River in Nevada, an asylum for the indigent insane of a state, a redevelopment grant for downtown Detroit, or a small grant to educate disabled children combined with a mandate to raise equal or greater local funds in Franklin, Maine (population 1,150) would be matters of "general Welfare" and thus properly within the scope of Congress' legislative powers.

If a majority of the citizens in each state agree with this reading of the Taxing for the General Welfare Clause, then Congress will, from year to year, expand its legislation in this direction.

A majority of the citizens of Franklin, Maine, however, voted in 1998 "to freeze their town's 1998/99 budget for special education to a symbolic $1 until the town's burgeoning special ed costs can be brought under control" (*The Wall Street Journal*, Review and Outlook, "Special Ed Rebels," September 8, 1998).

Thus we must answer today the same questions that were argued from the beginning of the Republic. Does the Constitution provide that Congress shall be the ultimate authority on education and the ultimate judge of the conscience of the people (by dictating the degree of sympathy to be given to the disabled)? Or does the Constitution leave stateside education, and the power to raise revenue for stateside education purposes, with the state and local governments?

The outcome depends on which of the two meanings of "equal protection" and of "general welfare" a majority of the citizens in each state will adopt.

Chapter IV

Housing

To be able to legislate about housing, Congress informally amended the Constitution and interpreted the "general welfare" as the welfare of any group Congress may choose.

During the first administration of President Franklin Roosevelt, Congress began to legislate with regard to private housing in the several states. The National Housing Act (Chapter 847, 48 Stat. 1246) became law on June 27, 1934. The Act contains few hints on which of its constitutional powers Congress relied for this legislation.

The main purposes of the act were to create federal insurance for private lending institutions which made home improvement loans or home loans, to create federal insurance for the savings accounts of private individuals in savings and loan associations, and to provide liquidity for the real estate financing market through so-called national mortgage associations, which bought first mortgages, pooled them and then issued and sold securities based on these pools of mortgages.

The act has been amended some 26 times since 1934. Additional functions were added. The Federal Housing Administration (1934 act) has been swallowed up by the Department of Housing and Urban Development. Over the decades, millions of Americans were helped to buy their homes with federally insured mortgages.

Yet where in the Constitution do we find Congress authorized to create a system for insuring loans made by private lending institutions, or insuring accounts held with private savings and loan associations? The powers "To borrow Money on the credit of the United States" and "To coin Money, [and] regulate the Value thereof" (Article I, Section 8, Clauses 2 and 5) on which Congress' banking legislation rests, appear to be the closest. But in the context of Article I, Section 8, the power to borrow money seems designed for carrying out the other functions enumerated in Section 8 rather than creating a scheme for insuring private financial instruments.

The New Deal has given us here one more informal amendment to the Constitution. Congress exercised a power that the great majority of the people, through their representatives, wanted to have exercised. And that exercise has been wholeheartedly approved for 65 years, or, at the very least, this power has not been substantially challenged during that period. I doubt that anyone would want to challenge it today.

But we should clearly recognize that it is an informal amendment to the Constitution made by Congress. It has proved a welcome amendment, but not all informal amendments to the Constitution which Congress may make in the years to come will necessarily be welcome. We should think about what we may do if ever we are faced with an unwelcome amendment.

By the Housing Act of 1949 (July 15, 1949, Chapter 338, Section 2, 63 Stat. 413; Title 42 USCA Section 1441) Congress broadened federal involvement in housing, particularly urban housing.

> The Congress declares that the general welfare and security of the Nation and the health and living standards of its people require housing production and related community development sufficient to remedy the serious housing shortage, the elimination of substandard and other inadequate housing through the clearance of slums and *blighted areas*, and the realization as soon as feasible of the goal of a decent home and a suitable environment for every American family, thus contributing to the development and redevelopment of communities and to the advancement of the growth, wealth and security of the Nation [42 USCA section 1441; emphasis added].

This purpose has been retained and strengthened in the Housing and Community Development Act of 1974 which, amended numerous times, is the law today (42 USCA Section 5301 et seq.).

The original mortgage insurance scheme was intended to stimulate the housing market. It left the judgment as to what home a person might afford to build or buy to that person and to the market.

With the Housing Act of 1949, the federal government began to determine what housing was "substandard" or otherwise "inadequate." This was done directly in federal urban renewal projects and indirectly by providing federal money to local authorities for clearing of slums and "blighted" areas. The local government determined what housing areas were to be considered "blighted," choosing some areas even when they were not slums and did not pose dangers to the public health or safety. A perfectly good, though perhaps antiquated, house located in a run-down neighborhood could be pulled down by the government (though with compensation payable) for no other purpose than to make the area, when rebuilt, look like the government wanted it to look.

This was a drastic change in the philosophy of American government. Instead of protecting individual choices of where to live, which did not interfere with the rights of others, the government began to decree how neighborhoods should look. The reference to "general welfare" in Section 1441 shows that Congress, in making this change in the philosophy of American government, meant to act here under its Spending Power ("collect Taxes ... to ... provide for the common Defence and general Welfare of the United States").

We have already briefly met with the Spending Power in the drinking age case (Chapter I, *South Dakota v. Dole*) and we have become aware of the ambiguity of the term "general welfare" (Chapter III). It is either, as in "common Defence and general Welfare," the defense and welfare of *all* Americans, nationwide; or it is the welfare of this or that individual or group, in this or that city, where, once the money has been expended for that individual or group, it adds to their welfare, and thereby adds to the sum total of goodness and welfare in the country, although there are millions of taxpayers for whose welfare it does nothing.

An interstate highway on which every American may travel by car or by bus is an example of the nationwide general welfare implicit in *common* defense and *general* welfare. But a redevelopment project in a large city could be "general" welfare only in the sense of adding to the total sum of goodness and well-being in the country. It does not potentially benefit every American. A community, which on its own, has taken care to prevent slums and blighted areas could not benefit from the availability of federal redevelopment money. Local self-reliance might even be discouraged by the availability of the federal money.

As in the context of education it will be up to the majority of the citizens in each state to choose which of the two meanings the constitutional phrase should be given.

We should keep in mind that "sum of goodness general welfare," since it does not have to be for *all* Americans, does not have any logical cutoff as to how many Americans are required to make the tax money they receive a part of the "general welfare." By pure logic, detached from common sense, a grant of a million dollars to one individual would raise the "sum of goodness general welfare" by one million dollars—if one does not ask where the money is coming from.

In the field of housing, it comes from the taxpayers, either directly, by way of congressional grants in aid to state or local agencies drawn from current federal revenue; or indirectly, by way of federal guaranty of redevelopment loans, for which the full faith and credit of the United States is pledged. For example, annual grants of $4 billion or more are contemplated by the Housing and Community Development Act (42 USCA Sections 5301(d), 5303). As the late Senator Dirksen of Illinois used to say, a billion here and a billion there, and pretty soon you are talking about real money.

The danger of "sum of goodness general welfare" is that it invites log rolling for pork barrel projects. Nationwide the taxpayers are asked to pay for the removal of "blighted areas" in this or that big city. The congressional representatives of those districts which cannot benefit from "urban renewal" will ask for equivalent federal spending in their districts as a condition for voting for the urban renewal spending, and so the pork is doled out in every direction. The need for many of the local federal programs is often doubtful, but the instinct of the politicians who ask for them is sound. They must do what they can for their constituents. When everybody's tax money is to flow to the big city for urban renewal for the general welfare, their constituents will ask, why don't we, the small town or rural people, get some share of the tax money for our "general welfare?" The inevitable answer has been "pork" legislation.

This result of the interpretation of the general welfare as the sum of "individual welfares" in various parts of the country was foreseen in the Founders' time. In 1817 Thomas Jefferson wrote:

> our tenet [position] ever was ... that Congress had not unlimited powers to provide for the general welfare, but were restrained to those [powers] specifically enumerated [Article I, Section 8]; and that ... it could not have been meant they should raise money for purposes which the enumeration did not place under their action...

Without the enumerated limits for the Spending Power, in Jefferson's view

> intrigue, negotiation, and the barter of votes might become as habitual in Congress, as they are in those legislatures [state legislatures] which have the appointment of officers, and which, with us [in Virginia], is called "logging," the term of the farmers for their exchanges of aid in rolling together the logs of their newly cleared grounds [Kurland, Vol. 2, p. 452, No. 25].

That is precisely where Congress is today.

We have it in our power to do away with this kind of spending, if we insist that the general welfare should be read in context as *common* defense and *general* welfare rather than out of context, as "sum of goodness general welfare."

The difference between the two readings is the difference between Big Government, with high federal taxes, and limited federal government, with lower taxes, as originally intended by the Founders. Limited federal government would leave the states free to collect taxes for truly needed projects, as distinguished from "pork" projects, undertaken mainly to bring back a share of federal tax money to each congressional district.

If, however, the majority of the citizens in each state believe that the present "sum of goodness" interpretation of the "general welfare" should be retained, then they must accept "pork barrel" legislation as an inevitable result of this interpretation. Congressional representatives must represent *their* districts. Therefore, if federal tax money is to be spent for purposes that do not benefit *all* Americans, congressmen must see to it that a fair share of the tax money flows into their districts.

Congress' involvement in housing in the several states brought with it also one informal judicial amendment to the Constitution. The Fifth Amendment provides: "nor shall private property be taken for public use, without just compensation."

The noun "use" has a great many nuanced meanings. The basic meaning is "the act of employing, using, or putting into service," and in law, "the enjoyment of property, as by the employment, occupation, or exercise of it" (*The Random House Dictionary of the English Language*, Unabridged Edition, 1967).

A "public use" would then be the use of a thing or a piece of land by the public. But land taken for redevelopment was not necessarily used by the public. In fact, the declaration of congressional policy in the Housing Act of 1949 stated that "private enterprise shall be encouraged to serve as large a part of the total need as it can" (42 USCA Section 1441). Urban redevelopment practice was frequently that the government would take private property located in a development zone from its owners, pay to the owners the "just compensation" required by the Constitution, clear the structures from it, and sell it to private persons who would build new structures on it, in accordance with the redevelopment plan. The new structures, in turn, would be used by other private persons who rented or bought them. Thus there was no "public use" in the plain English meaning of the term.

To accommodate urban redevelopment, the Constitution had to give. The watershed was crossed in a case involving a predecessor of the Housing Act of 1949, namely the District of Columbia Redevelopment Act of 1945 (60 Stat. 790). This act gave a redevelopment commission the power to take private property, with "just compensation" to the owners (known as the power of "eminent domain"), to be sold to other private persons who would rebuild it according to the development plan. The lower federal court considered this power to be unconstitutional, if applied to

> an urban area which does not breed disease or crime, is not a slum. Its fault is that it fails to meet what is called modern standards. Let us suppose that it is backward, stagnant, not properly laid out, economically Eighteenth Century—anything except detrimental to health, safety or morals. Suppose its owners and occupants like it that way ... suppose these people own these homes and can afford none more modern. The poor are entitled to own what they can afford [*Schneider v. District of Columbia* (1953) 117 F Supp 705, at p. 719].

The court said

> It is said that the established meaning of eminent domain includes measures for the "general welfare" and that new social doctrines have so enlarged the concept of public welfare as to include all measures designed for the public benefit. The difficulty lies ... in the practicality that some person ... must determine ... what is the public benefit. Therein lies the insuperable obstacle, in the American view. There is no more subtle means of transforming the basic concepts of our government, of shifting from the preeminence of individual rights to the preeminence of government wishes, than is afforded by redefinition of "general welfare," as that term is used to define the Government's power of seizure. If it were to be determined that it includes whatever a commission ... determines to be in the interest of "sound development," without definition of "sound development,"

> the ascendancy of government over the individual right to property will be complete ... We are of opinion that the Congress ... has no power to authorize the seizure ... of property for the sole purpose of redeveloping the area according to its ... judgment of what a well-developed, well-balanced neighborhood would be [117 F Supp at p. 720].

Here we are at the watershed. The lower federal court refused to cross. But, on appeal, the U.S. Supreme Court crossed the watershed:

> The concept of the public welfare is broad and inclusive ... The values it represents are spiritual as well as physical, aesthetic as well as monetary. It is within the power of the legislature to determine that the community should be beautiful as well as healthy, spacious as well as clean, well-balanced as well as carefully patrolled ... the power of eminent domain is merely the means to an end ... Here one of the means chosen is the use of private enterprise for redevelopment of the area ... the means of executing the project are for Congress and Congress alone to determine, once the public purpose has been established [*Berman v. Parker* (1954) 348 US 26, at p. 33, 99 L Ed 27, 75 S Ct 98].

Here the U.S. Supreme Court in effect amended the Fifth Amendment to read: nor shall private property be taken for *a public purpose* without just compensation.

To sum up, the expansion of congressional power to reach housing in the several states has brought with it:

1) Two informal amendments to the Constitution (first, congressional power to insure private financial instruments, and secondly, the change from public use to public purpose).

2) The "sum of goodness general welfare" interpretation of the Spending Power, which carries with it "pork barrel" legislation as a natural consequence.

We should be aware that this is the price we have paid for the federal involvement in housing. It will be up to the majority of the citizens in each state to decide whether we are willing to continue paying this price.

Chapter V

Americans with Disabilities

The Americans with Disabilities Act of 1990 is social legislation of the kind traditionally within the states' so-called "police power." Congress now has claimed this power for itself under the Commerce Clause, which it has extended even beyond its New Deal reach, and under the Enforcement Clause of the Fourteenth Amendment, which it has interpreted as giving Congress general legislative power. If the U.S. Supreme Court were to uphold this law as constitutional, there would no longer be a discernible limit to the power of Congress.

The Americans with Disabilities Act of 1990 is social legislation. Its central purpose is to prohibit discrimination against individuals with a physical or mental impairment which substantially limits one or more of their major life activities (Section 3, 104 Stat., at p. 329; 42 USCA Section 12102). Discrimination in employment and discrimination in public accommodations and services are the main targets.

In its "findings" Congress declared that discrimination against such individuals is "a serious and pervasive social problem," that people with disabilities "as a group, occupy an inferior status in our society, and that they are "a discrete and insular minority who have been faced with ... limitations ... beyond the control of such individuals" (Section 2, 104 Stat., at p. 328–329; 42 USCA Section 12101).

"Discrimination," as defined variously by Congress, broadly speaking consists of not hiring a disabled person who "with or without reasonable accommodation, can perform the essential functions of the employment position," and also consists of not adapting buildings, vehicles and telecommunications to make them usable by disabled persons. In addition to these adaptations, "reasonable accommodation" includes qualified interpreters for the hearing impaired, and qualified readers or taped texts and so forth for the visually impaired.

Broadly speaking, the Disabilities Act covers all employers of 15 or more persons (except the U.S. government) who are "engaged in an industry affecting commerce," all public services by state and or local government and by the National Railroad Passenger Corporation, and all private businesses which provide "public accommodations," "if the operations of such entities affect commerce." "Public accommodations" include hotels, restaurants, bars, movie theatres, lecture halls, bakeries, dry cleaners, shoe repair services, funeral parlors, museums, zoos, amusement parks, nurseries, private schools, day care centers, homeless shelters, gyms, golf courses, and so forth (Section 301, 104 Stat., at p. 354; 42 USCA Section 12181).

The Disabilities Act does not define what "affecting commerce" or "affect commerce" means, but Congress declared it to be its purpose

> to invoke the sweep of congressional authority, including the power to enforce the fourteenth amendment and to regulate commerce, in order to address the major areas of discrimination faced day-to-day by people with disabilities [Section 2, 104 Stat., at p. 329; 42 USCA Section 12101].

Congress has power "to regulate commerce ... among the several states" (Article I, Section 8, Clause 3). Congress also has power to enforce the Fourteenth Amendment by "appropriate legislation" (Fourteenth Amendment, Section 5). These two powers are supposed to authorize erecting this regulatory edifice over millions of private citizens.

Before we have a closer look at this proposed justification, we must acknowledge that the object of this legislation, to help disabled persons make a better life for themselves, is a worthy object. It grows directly out of the teachings of Christian ethics as they have come down over the centuries to the present day. In the ancient world, the disabled did not fare so well. For example, a Roman father of a family had the legal right to refuse to admit into the family a deformed or a female child. He had the choice of retroactive abortion; a rejected child would be exposed to die. (Will Durant, *The Story of Civilization*, Part III, *Caesar and Christ: A History of Roman Civilization and of Christianity from Their Beginnings to A.D. 325*, New York, Simon and Shuster, 1972, p. 56).

We also acknowledge that there are other worthy objects growing out of Christian ethics about which Congress might legislate. An example would be giving all your property to the poor, which if applied by law to every American would very likely "affect commerce." The question is not the worthiness of the legislative purpose, but whether the Constitution gives Congress the power to legislate about the matter in question.

The words of the Constitution, "to regulate Commerce ... among the several States," by themselves do not give any power to require the owner of a bakery employing 15 persons to build a wheelchair ramp next to some steps leading from the sidewalk to his store providing access for disabled customers, or to make such changes in his work area so that a person in a wheelchair could operate the bread making equipment. Such a bakery is not normally engaged in "Commerce ... among the several States." Since the power is not found in the words of the Constitution, it must come from an interpretation of the words.

We have seen that in the 1930s the power to regulate "commerce" was expanded by the legal fiction that you regulate commerce when you regulate local production, wages and working conditions, because goods so produced eventually may end up in the stream of commerce. The farmer who grew his own wheat to feed his livestock "affected commerce," because he reduced the demand for wheat by the amount he grew himself instead of buying it in the market (*Wickard v. Filburn* [1942] 317 US 111, 87 L Ed 122, 63 S Ct 82).

The manufacturer who paid some of his workers less than the federal minimum wage "affected commerce." The goods he produced at lower wage cost had a competitive advantage over goods produced paying the minimum wage, and thus could induce, in the absence of the minimum wage law, manufacturers in other states also to pay less than the minimum wage, thereby spreading substandard labor conditions (*U.S. v. Darby* [1941] 312 US 100, 85 L Ed 609, 61 S Ct 451).

How would our hypothetical baker "affect commerce" if he did *not* hire "an individual with a disability, who, with ... reasonable accommodation, can perform the essential functions of the employment position that such individual ... desires?" Would the bakery produce more bread, less bread, or the same amount, if the baker *did* hire the disabled person?

If the person, with some accommodation, *could* perform the essential functions of the employment, then hiring the person would not affect the bakery's output or prices. Thus hiring or not hiring would have no effect on the overall supply of bread in the country, unlike the farmer's case.

Would *not* hiring the disabled person create substandard labor conditions in another state, as in the minimum wage case? Not paying the minimum wage gave the employer there a competitive advantage which could cause employers in other states also to underpay their workers. But assuming, as Congress did, that the disabled person *can* perform the essential functions of the employment, *not* hiring such a person would not give our hypothetical baker a competitive advantage over bakers in other states because it would not increase his output or lower his costs. Hiring the disabled person and paying for the reasonable accommodations would reduce the baker's net income, because he would not be able to raise his prices without worsening his competitive position.

The minimum wage law forced *all* employers subject to it to pay the minimum wage. The Disabilities Act, however, forces only those bakers who receive a job application from a qualified disabled person to hire such persons. All other bakers, in all states, remain in their relative competitive position. Only the bakers who happen to receive the job application are put to the economic disadvantage of having their net income reduced by the cost of the "reasonable accommodations." You might even say that these bakers are denied the equal protection of the laws. Of all the bakers in their class, they only have to pay that extra cost. Their output of bread, and thus the nationwide output of bread, will remain unchanged. But they will have less net income than the bakers who received no job applications from disabled persons.

Thus the Disabilities Act is not a regulation of local economic activity that would, if unregulated, create adverse economic conditions in other states, as in the minimum wage law case. It is a law that randomly imposes economic disadvantages on individuals or business entities.

It is, therefore, fair to say that the Disabilities Act does not regulate activity, or the absence of activity, which "substantially affects" commerce among the several states. Thus to sustain it under the Commerce Clause, the legal fictions of the New Deal Amendment would have to be expanded further.

The Disabilities Act is social legislation. It dictates to the conscience of our hypothetical baker what he should do for the less fortunate in our society. You might say that it dictates Christian ethics to him. The goal of the Disabilities Act is worthy, but Congress does not, by a fair reading of the Commerce Clause even with the New Deal extensions, have power under that clause to regulate social conditions that have no substantial effect on commerce. So the act amounts to a new informal amendment to the Commerce Clause of the Constitution.

As the Chief Justice warned in *U.S. v. Lopez* (1995) 514 US 549, 131 L Ed 2d 626, at p. 641, 115 S Ct 1624, "depending on the level of generality, any activity can be looked upon as commercial."

Does Congress have power to make a general "police power" law like the Disabilities Act by way of "enforcing" the Fourteenth Amendment, which states, "nor shall any State ... deny to any person within its jurisdiction the equal protection of the laws" (Fourteenth Amendment, Section 1). Under Section 5. of the Fourteenth Amendment, Congress has power to enforce this provision by "appropriate legislation."

By the plain English meaning of its words, this section of the Fourteenth Amendment prohibits a *state* from denying equal protection of the laws. It does not prohibit *individuals* from doing anything.

What "laws" are meant? The phrase "within its jurisdiction" shows that it must be the laws which are or can be enforced in the courts of the state, the laws made by the state's legislature. As we have seen (Chapter III), a State may make laws which apply only to a segment or class of persons similarly situated, but within that class all must be treated the same way. As the U.S. Supreme court said "the function of the Equal Protection Clause ... is simply to measure the validity of classifications created by *state laws...*" (*San Antonio Independent School District v. Rodriguez* [1973] 411 US 1, 36 L Ed 2d 16, at p. 58, 93 S Ct 1278 (emphasis added).

Nothing in the words of the Fourteenth Amendment indicates what level of protection a state must give, what protective laws a State must enact. Congress has the power to force the states to apply with an even hand whatever protective laws the states have chosen to enact. But the words of the Amendment by their plain English meaning do not give Congress a power to create new constitutional rights in the name of "equal protection of the laws." It would take considerable "interpretation" to do that.

The States have the "whole power of legislation" (*The Federalist*, Nos. 32, 33, 41, 55, 83 [1787]). Congress has only the powers enumerated in the Constitution (see Chapter I). The "whole power" includes the so-called police power of the states, which is the power to legislate about health, welfare, morals, social relations, and so on. This power of the states is limited only by the U.S. Constitution where applicable, and by the states' own constitutions. The States would have power to enact social legislation like the Disabilities Act, and some have done so. But, under the plain English meaning of the words of the Constitution, without further informal amendment, Congress does not have such a power.

By the Disabilities Act Congress has purported to give to disabled persons legal rights against their fellow citizens which have no basis in the Constitution. By the Act, Congress prohibits "discrimination" against the disabled, by anyone. But the Fourteenth Amendment does not contain the word "discrimination," it prohibits *states*, but nobody else, from denying to anyone equal protection of the laws state legislatures make. You might say that it thus prohibits *states* from "discriminating" against people by means of state laws, but there is still no word in the text of the Fourteenth Amendment that prohibits private individuals from doing anything.

The Disabilities Act not only obligates private persons to hire qualified disabled persons, it commands them to pay for "reasonable accommodations" for these persons. As stated before, Congress' aim is worthy, but does the Constitution really give such a power to Congress?

Have the courts interpreted the Equal Protection of the Laws Clause and the Enforcement Clause of the Fourteenth Amendment to find such a congressional power?

The question whether Congress has the power to "enforce" the Equal Protection of the Laws Clause by requiring states and private individuals to hire qualified disabled persons and to change buildings, buses and trains to accommodate the disabled has not yet come before the U.S. Supreme Court.

In the lower federal courts there have been decisions upholding Congress' power to enact the Disabilities Act, and decisions denying that power. For example, one district court took the view that

> the statute [the Disabilities Act] does not elevate the disabled to a status above others; rather the reasonable accommodation requirement and other affirmative obligations allow the disabled to achieve equal status [*Martin v. State of Kansas* (1997) 978 F Supp 992, at p. 996].

Another district court concluded

> The [Disabilities Act] … seeks to single out the disabled for special, advantageous treatment. In other words, the [Disabilities Act] demands entitlements to achieve its goals. This is beyond the purview of the Enforcement Clause [Section 5 of the Fourteenth Amendment] as the concept of entitlements has little to do with promoting the "equal protection of the laws" [*Brown v. North Carolina Division of Motor Vehicles* (1997) 987 F Supp 451, at p. 458].

Yet another district court said

> Congress cannot stretch Section 5 and the Equal Protection Clause of the Fourteenth Amendment to force a state to provide allegedly *equal* treatment by guaranteeing *special* treatment or "accommodation" for disabled persons [*Garrett v. Board of Trustees of the University of Alabama* (1998) 989 F Supp 1409, at p. 1410. *Note:* The U.S. Supreme Court has accepted this case for review, but only on the question whether the Eleventh Amendment to the US Constitution prohibits suits based on the Disabilities Act in federal court by private citizens against nonconsenting States. *Board of Trustees of the University of Alabama v. Garrett* (2000) 529 US 1065, 146 L Ed 2d 479, 120 S Ct 1669].

Curiously these courts, both upholding Congress' power and denying it, rely on the same U.S. Supreme Court precedent, *City of Boerne v. Flores* (1997) 521 US 507, 138 L Ed 2d 624, 117 S Ct 2157. In that case the Court held that Congress' power to enforce Section 1 of the Fourteenth Amendment (including the Due Process Clause and the Equal Protection Clause) is "remedial," meaning Congress could only remedy or prevent unconstitutional actions and measures of the States, it could not make "a substantive change in the governing law" (*City of Boerne* 138 L Ed 2d, at p. 638).

This is the concept under which some of the lower federal courts denied Congress' power to create the Disabilities Act entitlements. (See e.g., *Brown*, 987 F Supp, at p. 456.)

But, in the *City of Boerne* case the Supreme Court also said:

> Legislation which deters or remedies constitutional violations can fall within the sweep of Congress' enforcement power even if in the process it prohibits conduct which is not itself unconstitutional and intrudes into "legislative spheres of autonomy previously reserved to the States" [*City of Boerne* 138 L Ed 2d, at p. 637].

This is the concept some of the lower federal courts have used to uphold the provisions of the Disabilities Act which traditionally could only be a matter of state "police power." (See e.g., *Martin*, 978 F Supp, at p. 996.)

The U.S. Supreme Court in *City of Boerne* held that Congress' enforcement power was intended to be "remedial" only, which is to say Congress could by legislation give a remedy to persons whose rights had been denied by a state law.

For this holding the Court relied on the history of the Fourteenth Amendment. The first draft of the Fourteenth Amendment presented to the House of Representatives in 1866 by Representative John Bingham of Ohio stated:

> The Congress shall have power to make all laws which shall be necessary and proper to secure to the citizens of each State all privileges and immunities of citizens in the several States, and to all persons in the several States equal protection in the rights of life, liberty and property [*City of Boerne* 138 L Ed 2d, at p. 639].

This draft was known as the Bingham proposal. It was rejected by the House. The tenor of the objections was that it would radically change the federal design of the Constitution, there would not be much left for the State legislatures, it would work an entire change in our government, and so forth. (*City of Boerne* 138 L Ed 2d, at p. 639–640). Instead of the Bingham proposal the present Fourteenth Amendment was eventually proposed. "The revised Amendment proposal did not raise the concerns expressed earlier regarding broad congressional power to prescribe uniform national laws with respect to life, liberty, and property" (*City of Boerne* 138 L Ed 2d, at p. 640).

The revised Amendment proposal, which became the Fourteenth Amendment, allowed Congress to correct state laws which denied or abridged the rights given by the Fourteenth Amendment, but Congress was not to be given the power of the Bingham proposal to create new rights by legislation.

The rejection of the Bingham proposal also served to maintain the traditional separation of powers between Congress and the Judiciary. The Bingham proposal would have given Congress the power

> to interpret and elaborate on the meaning of the new Amendment through legislation. Under it, "Congress, and not the courts, was to judge whether or not any of the privileges or immunities were not secured to citizens in the several States" [*City of Boerne* 138 L Ed 2d, at p. 641].

Since the Bingham proposal was rejected, "[t]he power to interpret the Constitution in a case or controversy remains in the Judiciary" (*City of Boerne* 138 L Ed 2d, at p. 641).

The *City of Boerne* case involved Congress' enforcement power of the Fourteenth Amendment with regard to the Due Process of Law Clause.

The Court has not yet had an opportunity to consider this enforcement power as applied to the Equal Protection of the Laws Clause. The Court is aware of the risk to the basic structure of our government that would result from letting Congress interpret the enforcement power given by the Fourteenth Amendment as a power to legislate generally about life, liberty, and property throughout the United States:

> If Congress could define its own powers by altering the Fourteenth Amendment's meaning, no longer would the Constitution be "superior paramount law, unchangeable by ordinary means." It would be "on a level with ordinary legislative acts, and, like other acts, ... alterable when the legislature shall please to alter it." ... Under this approach, it is difficult to conceive of a principle that would limit congressional power [*City of Boerne* 138 L Ed 2d, at p. 644].

So we are standing near another watershed. When enough Disabilities Act cases will have worked their way through the federal court system, the Supreme Court will have to decide whether the enforcement power of Section 5 of the Fourteenth Amendment authorizes Congress to create rights and duties for private individuals in the name of congressionally determined equal protection, or whether the words of the Fourteenth Amendment "nor shall any *State* ... deny" (emphasis added) retain their meaning.

If Congress had power to determine by federal laws what "equal protection of the laws" is, or is not, it is obvious that state legislatures would become irrelevant. Federal law is supreme (U.S. Constitution, Article VI, Clause 2), and if Congress, to pick but one example, had power to determine that single family residential zoning denies equal protection of the laws to people who want to build a high rise apartment building in a nice suburb and rent it to the poor, that would be the end of such zoning.

Practically all laws of a state classify people in some way, and each of these classifications would, on the grounds of equal protection of the laws, then be in the power of Congress to change. In the watershed case, when it comes before the Supreme Court, the Court will have the choice to adhere to the remnants of the traditional concept of a federal government limited to enumerated powers, or to bow to Congress and allow

Congress to legislate without limit. If the latter, we, the citizens, will have to make up our minds, whether we agree to have our traditional government of a federal union of the states changed to a government in which the states will merely be administrative organs of the central government in Washington, D.C.

Chapter VI

Air

Congress has extended the New Deal Amendments' fiction that Congress regulates "commerce" when in fact it regulates local production, labor conditions, and so forth, to the point where almost any "nationwide" problem can be regulated as "commerce." So air pollution, a public health problem, was regulated because air "affects commerce." To achieve air pollution control, Congress required the states to enact legislation satisfactory to the Environmental Protection Agency (EPA). Congress stopped, barely, short of giving the EPA the power to compel the states to enact such legislation, but at least one court of appeals actually found such a power in the statute.

Congress began to legislate regarding air pollution in 1955. The enactment followed the pattern set by the Clean Water Act of 1948:

AN ACT to provide research and technical assistance relating to air pollution control.

> ... in recognition of the dangers to the *public health and welfare* ... and hazards to air and ground *transportation*, from air pollution, it is hereby declared to be the policy of Congress to preserve and protect the primary responsibilities and rights of the States and local governments in controlling air pollution, to support and aid technical research ... and to provide Federal technical services and financial aid to State and local government air pollution control agencies [69 Stat. 322, July 14, 1955; emphasis added].

Congress appears to have been uncertain about its power to enter the field. Public health traditionally had been a matter for the states. So Congress reaffirmed the states' powers, but called them "primary," and thereby found a "secondary" role for itself. Congress was merely going to help the states to control air pollution by technical assistance and some financial aid. Presumably this was "spending" for the "general welfare." "Transportation," on the other hand, involves the Commerce

Clause with the power to regulate rather than merely help. The surgeon general of the United States was to administer the program.

This first program was expanded by several enactments during the 1960s. But by 1970 little progress to control air pollution had been made, and as the Supreme Court described it, "Congress reacted by taking a stick to the States in the form of the Clean Air Amendments of 1970" (*Train v. Natural Resources Defense Council* [1975] 421 US 60, 43 L Ed 2d 731, at p. 737, 95 S Ct 1470). Under the 1970 law the states were, for the first time, *required* to meet specified air quality standards within a defined time period. Congress began to regulate air quality. Where in the Constitution is that power given to Congress?

"Commerce" takes place through the *air* and within the *air*. There are four kinds of air: clean air, semipolluted air, polluted air, and unbreathable air. It is a violation of... to release into clean *air* ... and so on. Sounds familiar?

Our air needed to be cleaned up. The problem transcends state lines in many regions of the United States. There needed to be a power in the national legislature to deal with it. Eighty years ago this power would have been created by an amendment to the Constitution, as was Prohibition, because, just as by the plain English words of the Constitution, no power to prohibit the manufacture and sale of liquor was given, so no power to regulate ambient air quality nationwide is given by the text of the Constitution.

The legal fiction of the New Deal Amendment, that you regulate commerce among the several states when you regulate local conditions that may affect it, came to the rescue.

Without air there could be no commerce, therefore air affects commerce (a facetious statement). This reasoning was not actually used by a court. Instead, no reasoning at all was used. In *United States v. Ohio Department of Highway Safety* (1980) 635 F 2d 1195, at p. 1205, the court simply stated that the clean air legislation "represents a lawful exercise by Congress of its power to regulate interstate commerce."

The court was aided by the State of Ohio in using this shortcut: "The State of Ohio does not dispute the fact that air pollution is a national problem and that its control by Congress is within the authority granted by the Commerce Clause" (635 F 2d, at p. 1204).

Once a problem has been described as "national" it apparently automatically "affects commerce." Here we have a further extension of the legal fiction of the New Deal Amendment. By now the Commerce Clause reads more like: The Congress shall have power ... to regulate commerce with foreign nations and with the Indian tribes, and to regulate *any nationwide problem, including* commerce.

The U.S. Supreme Court declined to review the *Ohio* case (451 US 949, 68 L Ed 2d 334, 101 S Ct 2031 [1981]). This does not mean that the Court approved of the case, but merely that the question remains open. Every year the Court declines to review hundreds of cases without comment.

In a more recent case in the same judicial circuit as the *Ohio* case, the court of appeals said:

> It is undisputed that air pollution is a severe national problem. Congress has exercised its power under the Commerce Clause to regulate directly air pollution [*Dressman v. Costle* (1985) 759 F 2d 548, at p. 556].

The incantation of the words "national problem" and "Commerce Clause" was apparently felt sufficient to establish Congress' power to regulate. Not a word was said about just how air pollution, a public health problem, substantially affects commerce among the several states.

Besides the Commerce Clause question, the Clean Air Act presents a second constitutional problem. Assuming that Congress has power to regulate air pollution, does Congress have power to force the states to legislate or to make regulations about air quality as prescribed by Congress?

By the traditional interpretation of the Constitution, federal legislation regulating commerce *replaces* or supersedes state legislation on the same subject. Traditionally Congress has had power to regulate directly the conduct of individuals or business entities engaged in commerce, but it does not have the power to compel the states to regulate commerce through state legislation prescribed by Congress.

The Clean Air Act changed that pattern. It requires the States to "adopt and submit to the [Environmental Protection Agency] ... a plan which provides for implementation, maintenance, and enforcement" (42 USCA Section 7410[a]) of federally determined air quality standards. The state's plan must "provide ... necessary assurances that the State ... will have adequate personnel, funding, and authority *under State ... law* to carry out such implementation plan" (42 USCA Section 7410[a][2][E]; emphasis added).

And the state's plan must "provide for revision of such plan ... whenever the [EPA] ... finds that the plan is substantially inadequate to attain the national ambient air quality standard" (42 USCA Section 7410[a][2][H]).

How can a state "adopt" such a plan? Only by having it enacted into law by the state legislature. Under a state constitution a state governor or a state judge would not normally have the power to adopt such a plan.

Here Congress departed from the basic concept of our federal union inherent in the Constitution, namely that the national government acts *"directly upon the citizens,"* and not, as under the Articles of Confederation, upon the states (*New York v. United States* [1992] 505 US 144, 120 L Ed 2d 120, at p. 141, 112 S Ct 2408).

In the Clean Air Act, as shown by the quotes from Section 7410, Congress told the states what legislation they must adopt and what amounts of tax money they must set aside to enforce this legislation once accepted.

How was this novel congressional command to be enforced against the states? In the provisions for federal enforcement (42 USCA Section 7413) Congress avoided clearly overstepping the line, but left enough ambiguity so that the courts might solve this problem for Congress.

Section 7413 specifies three methods of enforcement against persons who violate the air quality standards:

1) orders issued by the EPA which may provide for monetary penalties;

2) civil court actions for injunction and monetary penalties;

3) criminal penalties such as fines or imprisonment.

These can be used against "any person" who has violated any requirement of an "applicable implementation plan." For criminal prosecution the violation must have been "knowingly."

Subsection (a)(2) of Section 7413 creates a special procedure for situations where the violations are "so widespread that [they] appear to result from a failure of the State in which the plan ... applies to enforce the plan effectively..." In such a case the EPA must notify the state about the widespread violations. If the violations continue for more than 30 days after that, the EPA must give "public notice" of that fact. After that the EPA may take enforcement action directly, against "any person," until the State satisfies the EPA that the state will properly enforce the law.

This statute does not seem to provide for any action by the EPA directly against the state. The state is to be kept informed. If the state doesn't act within 30 days, then "public notice" is given and the EPA takes over. But there is an ambiguity. Is a state a "person?" If so, then the statute could be read to authorize the EPA to sue the state in federal court. But if the statute is read that way, then the state could also be subject to criminal prosecution as a "person who knowingly violates any requirement ... of an applicable implementation plan." That seems absurd.

Several federal courts of appeals concluded that the statute would be unconstitutional, if it were read this way. These decisions came before the U.S. Supreme Court in one consolidated case (*EPA v. Brown* [1977] 431 US 99, 52 L Ed 2d 166, 97 S Ct 1635). But before the Supreme Court, the EPA suddenly no longer claimed that a state could be compelled to enact laws or regulations about air quality and told the Court that it needed to modify the regulations it had tried to enforce in its lawsuits against the states.

The Supreme Court vacated the judgments and sent the cases back to the courts of appeals for new decisions after the proposed modifications of the regulations by the EPA.

Three years later the question of forcing a state to enact regulations came up again in *United States v. Ohio Department of Highway Safety* (1980) 635 F 2d 1195. The EPA had found an air quality implementation plan of the state of Ohio not adequate, and as permitted by the Clean Air Act, the EPA supplemented the state plan by publishing a regulation which required enforcement by way of denying registration renewal to offending cars. The director of the Ohio Highway Safety Department had no authority under Ohio law to deny registration renewal for noncomplying vehicles, and refused to do so. The EPA sued the state in federal court.

The trial judge dismissed the suit, holding that the EPA should have proceeded under the subsection which deals with "widespread" violations. Remember, under that part of the statute the EPA must notify the state, wait 30 days, then give "public notice," and then go after the violators itself.

But the court of appeals held that the state, under the plan, had "the obligation to prevent use of the [highways] by noncomplying vehicles. When the State fails to perform that duty it becomes a person in violation of a requirement of the implementation plan" (635 F 2d at p. 1204). Being a "person" in violation, the court held, the state can be sued directly by the EPA. One judge dissented: "It would ... violate the plainest principles of federalism ... The State should no more be required to enforce federal laws than the federal government should be required to enforce state laws" (635 F 2d at p. 1206).

The US Supreme Court declined to review the case (*U.S. v Ohio Department...* (1981) 451 US 949, 68 L Ed 2d 334, 101 S Ct 2031). When the Supreme Court declines to review a decision, this does not mean that it approves, or disapproves, of the decision. The decision remains in force as a binding federal precedent in the judicial circuit of the court of appeals that has rendered it. In the *Ohio* case, this is the Sixth Circuit, consisting of the states of Tennessee, Kentucky, Ohio, and Michigan.

In the *EPA v. Brown* case the Supreme Court had avoided deciding the question of Congress' power to force states to legislate. Now it avoided it again. Why? We can only speculate. The Court was faced with a Congress dead set to regulate air quality. The matter was perceived as urgent. There probably would have been an outcry if the Court had told Congress that Congress had no constitutional power to compel the states to enact air pollution legislation prescribed by Congress. The Court might have been browbeat and forced to escape into yet another legal fiction, as had happened at the time of the New Deal Amendment.

Whatever the reason, the Court bided its time and made the point forcefully on two later occasions, in other contexts.

In *New York v. United States* (1992) 505 US 144, 120 L Ed 2d 120, 112 S Ct 2408, striking down several provisions of the Low Level Radioactive Waste Policy Amendments Act of 1985, the Court said:

> While Congress has substantial powers to govern the Nation directly, including in areas of intimate concern to the States, the Constitution has never been understood to confer upon Congress the ability to require the States to govern according to Congress' instructions [120 L Ed 2d, at p. 141].

And further:

the Constitution protects us from our own best intentions: it divides power among sovereigns and among branches of government precisely so that we may resist the temptation to concentrate power in one location as an expedient solution to the crisis of the day. The shortage of disposal sites for radioactive waste is a pressing national problem, but a judiciary that licensed extra-constitutional government with each issue of comparable gravity would, in the long run, be far worse.

States are not mere political subdivisions of the United States. State governments are neither regional offices nor administrative agencies of the Federal Government [120 L Ed 2d, at p. 158].

More recently, the Court confirmed this view of the Constitution. In *Printz v. United States* (1997) 521 US 898, 138 L Ed 2d 914, 117 S Ct 2365, the Court struck down provisions of the Brady Handgun Violence Prevention Act which purported to compel local law enforcement officers to do background checks required by the Act. The Court said: "The Federal Government may not compel the States to enact or administer a federal regulatory program" (138 L Ed 2d, at p. 943).

In summation, the legal fiction that Congress is regulating commerce among the several states when it is regulating air quality nationwide stands undisturbed. Commerce takes place in air, therefore...

The requirement that states must enact into law such air pollution control plans as satisfy the EPA is still on the statute books, and the states have complied. But in the light of the *New York* case and the *Printz* case, will the EPA again sue a state to force it to enact laws or regulations?

Our air is cleaner, but our federal system under which the state governments and the national government are each sovereign within the sphere assigned to them has taken a beating. We enjoy the cleaner air, but we should not close our eyes to the price we paid for it.

Chapter VII

Water

As in the case of air pollution, Congress used the fiction of the New Deal Amendment, that you regulate interstate commerce when you regulate local conditions, to create for itself a power to regulate any "nationwide" problem. To achieve water pollution control Congress required the states to legislate control measures, subject to approval by federal agencies, and if not approved, to be superseded by federal regulations which the states must then enforce.

Congress began to legislate regarding water pollution even earlier than air pollution. The statute is commonly referred to as the Clean Water Act. Its first version dates to June 30, 1948:

> in connection with the exercise of jurisdiction over the *waterways* of the Nation and in consequence of the benefits resulting to the *public health and welfare* by the abatement of stream pollution, it is hereby declared to be the policy of Congress to recognize, preserve and protect the *primary responsibilities and rights of the States* in controlling water pollution, to ... aid technical research ... and to provide Federal technical services ... and financial aid [62 Stat. 1155; emphasis added].

The reference to "waterways" shows that Congress had the Commerce Clause in mind. Navigation traditionally has been regulated under that clause. The reference to "welfare" and to "financial aid" hints at the Spending Clause (collect Taxes ... for the ... general Welfare) but in substance the Clean Water Act was a public health measure. The surgeon general of the United States was to administer this law.

Public health had traditionally been a matter in the states' jurisdiction. Congress acknowledged this fact by the reference to "rights of the States," but opened the door to federal intrusion by the words "primary" and "responsibilities." What had historically been a matter of all power with the states and no power with the union, now became primary power of the states and secondary power of the union. And there was the reference to "responsibilities." Somebody had to determine if the States were discharging their responsibilities. If Congress had secondary responsibility, naturally Congress would step in when the states "failed." The camel's nose was under the tent at this point.

By 1972 the Clean Water Act had been amended some 12 times. But Congress felt that insufficient progress had been made in cleaning up the nation's waters and enacted a comprehensive scheme of water pollution control, the Federal Water Pollution Control Act Amendments of 1972 (86 Stat. 816; 33 USCA Section 1251 et seq.; the amended law is still commonly referred to as the Clean Water Act).

> The Amendments established a new system of regulation under which it is illegal for anyone to discharge pollutants into the Nation's waters except pursuant to a permit.... To the extent that the Environmental Protection Agency, charged with administering the Act, has promulgated regulations establishing specific effluent limitations, those limitations are incorporated as conditions of the permit.... Permits are issued either by the EPA or by a qualifying state agency [*City of Milwaukee v. Illinois* (1981) 451 US 304, 68 L Ed 2d 114, at p. 122, 101 S Ct 1784].

The constitutional problems with the Clean Water Act in its current form are similar to those of the Clean Air Act.

First, by the text of the Constitution, no power is given to Congress to regulate water pollution, a public health problem. To find the power, you have to interpret the power to regulate commerce among the several states as a power to protect public health. Under the Commerce Clause, Congress has power over the nation's navigable waters, because navigation has traditionally been considered a part of commerce. "All America understands, and has uniformly understood, the word 'commerce' to comprehend navigation" (Kurland, Vol. 2, p. 498, No. 16, *Gibbons v. Ogden* [1824]). But whether the waters plied by steamers or barges are clean or dirty is not a matter of commerce, but of public health and of aesthetics. So the fiction of the New Deal Amendment would have to be extended to hold that polluted water affects navigation—because barge crews cannot drink water out of the river? because the barges have to be painted more often? because pollution deters pleasure boating?

Remember the schoolboy's exam reasoning: Commerce, in the form of navigation, takes place on *water*. There are four kinds of *water*: clean *water*, semi-polluted *water*, polluted *water*, poisonous *water*. It is a violation of ... to release ... into *water*....

It is left up to you to find a more convincing logical connection. In the courts, as we shall see, the problem of a logical connection to commerce has been solved by not asking the question.

As to the second constitutional problem, the Clean Water Act, after laying down the general rule for the entire nation that "the discharge of any pollutant by any person shall be unlawful," compels the states to enact water quality standards, subject to approval by the EPA in accordance with federal standards determined by the EPA pursuant to the act (86 Stat., at p. 844, Section 301; 33 USCA Section 1311).

Thus, as in the case of the Clean Air Act, Congress created a regulatory scheme which the states are compelled to carry into effect by state legislation. The enforcement provisions of the Clean Water Act are similar to those of the Clean Air Act, but go farther in one respect: A State is made liable for the payment of penalties incurred by a municipality in the state "to the extent that the laws of the State prevent the municipality from raising revenues needed" to pay such penalties (33 USCA Section 1319[e]).

The States have largely complied with the Clean Water Act. No case challenging the overall constitutionality of the act has reached the United States Supreme Court. As in the case of the Clean Air Act, the challenge could have been that Congress does not have power to regulate in the first place, and that even if Congress had such power, it could only exercise it by superseding state laws with federal laws and federal enforcement, not by compelling the states to make and enforce regulations as if the states were regional offices of the EPA.

A few lower federal court decisions have upheld some of the enforcement provisions of the Clean Water Act as constitutional (*United States v. Duracell International, Inc.* [1981] 510 FS 154; *United States v. District of Columbia* [1981] 654 F 2d 802).

But, in recent years the United States Supreme Court has firmly stated that "The Federal government may not compel the States to enact or administer a federal regulatory program (*Printz v. United States* [1997] 521 US 898, 138 L Ed 2d 914, at p. 943, 117 S Ct 2365).

And that "the Constitution has never been understood to confer upon Congress the ability to require the States to govern according to Congress' instructions" (*New York v. United States* [1992] 505 US 144, 120 L Ed 2d 120, at p. 141, 112 S Ct 2408).

At the present time these statements of principle coexist with two federal regulatory schemes which do exactly what the Court said the Constitution forbids: The Clean Air Act and the Clean Water Act, in substance, have compelled the states to enact and administer federal regulatory programs. It is a legal fiction to say that the states are acting on their own in enacting water quality standards when these are invalid unless approved by the EPA. (Section 303, 86 Stat. at pp. 846–847; 33 USCA Section 1313.)

We have previously briefly explored the connection between navigation, being a part of commerce, and the quality of the water on which navigation takes place, which is a public health and an aesthetics question. We found it hard to establish a logical connection between navigable water and clean water, except by reasoning: Navigation, a part of commerce, takes place on water. People need clean water to drink. Therefore, without clean water there cannot be commerce by navigation. Thus clean water substantially affects commerce and Congress has power under the Commerce Clause to regulate water pollution in the navigable waters of the United States. Convincing logic, is it not?

But environmental concerns do not stop where a river ceases to be navigable, which is where, theoretically, congressional power to regulate commerce stops. Instead of recognizing the need for creating, by formal constitutional amendment, a congressional power to deal with nationwide environmental concerns, Congress removed the obstacle by simply dropping the word "navigable" from its definition of the scope of its jurisdiction.

> (7) The term "navigable waters" means *the waters of the United States,* including the territorial seas [33 USCA Section 1362(7); emphasis added].

This definition left open the question whether Congress had given itself power to regulate every drop of water on, around, within, under, and above the United States, or whether this boot-strapped power has any limits. Congress left it to the EPA and the Corps of Engineers, the administrative agencies charged with carrying the law into effect, to answer this question.

The Corps of Engineers came out with a regulation defining "waters of the United States," which included all navigable waters that had traditionally been subject to Congress' powers. Also included were

> (3) All *other waters* such as intrastate lakes, rivers, streams (including intermittent streams) mudflats, sandflats, wetlands, sloughs, prairie potholes, wet meadows, playa lakes, or natural ponds, *the use, degradation or destruction of which could affect interstate or foreign commerce* including any such waters:
>
> > (i) Which are or could be used by interstate or foreign travelers for recreational or other purposes; or
> > (ii) From which fish or shellfish are or could be taken and sold in interstate or foreign commerce; or
> > (iii) Which are or could be used for industrial purposes by industries in interstate commerce.
>
> [33 CFR Section 328.3(a). See also 40 CFR Section 230.3(s)(3) (EPA's identical definition). As quoted in: *Leslie Salt Company v. United States* (1995) 55 F 3d 1388, at p. 1391; emphasis added].

"Wetlands," in turn, were defined as

> The term "wetlands" means those areas that are inundated or saturated by surface or ground water at a frequency and duration sufficient to support, and that under normal circumstances do support, a prevalence of vegetation typically adapted for life in saturated soil conditions. Wetlands generally include swamps, marshes, bogs and similar areas [33 CFR Section 323.2(c) (1978). As quoted in *United States v. Riverside Bayview Homes, Inc.* (1985) 474 US 121, 88 L Ed 2d 419, at p. 424, 106 S Ct 455].

In the *Riverside Bayview Homes* case the Corps' regulations were challenged on the ground that since Congress used the word "waters of the United States" in the statute, Congress did not mean to include lands. Hence the Corps' regulation which defined "wetlands" as being "waters of the United States" was going beyond the law Congress had enacted.

Curiously, Congress' expansion of its commerce power from navigable waters, on which commerce does take place, to waters without commerce in the form of navigation, was not challenged. Apparently the legal fiction of the New Deal Amendment was so well established that the mere recital that the "use, degradation or destruction" of the "other waters" *could affect* commerce was felt to be sufficient to give Congress the power to regulate these waters in any manner it chose.

The Court upheld the Corps' regulation which defined "water" as including "wet land" as a reasonable interpretation of the statute:

> the evident breadth of congressional concern for protection of water quality and aquatic ecosystems suggests that it is reasonable for the Corps to interpret the term "waters" to encompass wetlands *adjacent to waters as more conventionally* defined [*United States v. Riverside Bayview Homes, Inc.* (1985) 474 US 121, 88 L Ed 2d 419, at p. 430, 106 S Ct 455; emphasis added].

The basic underlying constitutional question, what "water quality" and "aquatic ecosystems" have to do with "Commerce ... among the several States" was not discussed.

If by the Constitution the people meant to specify the limits of the federal government's power, then the words of the Constitution must be given the meaning generally understood by the people, otherwise Congress cannot be kept within its limits. The legal fiction of the New Deal Amendment that commerce includes everything that could affect commerce is severely eroding the Constitution.

By the text of the regulations, water includes adjacent land; and commerce includes a swim by a foreign tourist in a prairie pothole. Thus, with the approval of Congress and the Court, the normal English meaning of "commerce" has been stretched beyond recognition. The next step was to reach "wetlands" that were not adjacent to any body of water.

The case of *Leslie Salt Company v. United States* (1995) 55 F 3d 1388, involved a parcel of land near a slough which was connected to San Francisco Bay. The land had previously been used for producing salt and there were on it man-made shallow basins for crystallizing salt and man-made pits for collecting calcium chloride. Salt production had been discontinued.

> During much of the year, these areas were dry. During the winter and spring, however, rainwater creates temporary ponds. Migratory birds use these ponds for habitat. The dispute ... began in 1985, when Leslie Salt began digging a feeder ditch and a siltation pond on its property and began discharging fill that affected the seasonally ponded areas [55 F 3d, at p. 1391].

Landfill is defined by the Clean Water Act as a pollutant (33 USCA Section 1362(6)). The Corps of Engineers asserted that the company needed a permit for placing the fill. The company asserted that its man-made salt crystallizing basins and pits were not "other waters" under the regulation.

The court of appeals held that the basins and pits were "other waters" and that the "commerce clause power, and thus the Clean Water Act, is broad enough to extend the Corps' jurisdiction to local waters which may provide habitat to migratory birds and endangered species" (55 F 3d, at p. 1392).

The Court relied on a precedent case to the effect that it was reasonable to interpret the regulation

> as allowing migratory birds to form the connection between "other waters" and interstate commerce. The court noted that millions of dollars are spent on hunting, trapping, and observing migratory birds, and that the destruction of wetlands impinges on that commerce [55 F 3d, at p. 1393–1394].

The legal fiction of the New Deal Amendment holds that when an activity, a thing, or a geographical feature, could affect commerce, then Congress may regulate it. But does it follow that Congress may regulate every aspect of it, or only such aspects as affect commerce?

In the example of the isolated, seasonal ponds, the link to commerce was said to be the migratory birds. Filling in their seasonal habitat was assumed to affect commerce and give Congress power to regulate the fill.

But what if the landowner had deepened and widened the ponds to create a year-round habitat for ducks, so that the result of the earth-moving operation would not have "impinged" on commerce, there being no diminution of duck habitat? You would think that in such a case Congress would have no power to regulate the earthmoving. You are wrong. The government has actually sent a man to federal prison for building duck ponds on "wetlands" (James Bovard, *Lost Rights: The Destruction of American Liberty*, St. Martin's Press, New York, 1994, p. 36).

The reason given was that "wetlands" have unique vegetation. So they do, but where is the link between "Commerce ... among the several States" and that vegetation?

The United States Supreme Court declined to review the *Leslie Salt* case. One justice believed that the Commerce Clause had been stretched too far by the "migratory bird rule."

> Apparently the Corps' regulations are based on the assumption, improper in my opinion, that the self-propelled flight of birds across

state lines creates a sufficient interstate nexus to justify the Corps' assertion over any standing water that could serve as a habitat for migratory birds ... the Corps' expansive interpretation ... may test the very "bounds of reason" ... and, in my mind, likely stretches Congress' Commerce Clause powers beyond the breaking point [*Cargill, Inc. v. United States* (1995) 516 US 955, 133 L Ed 2d 325, at p. 327, 116 S Ct 407 Cargill, Inc., is the successor in interest of Leslie Salt Co.].

This is where the Commerce Clause stands today, thanks to the legal fiction of the New Deal Amendment that everything which *could affect* commerce is subject to Congress' power.

Eighty years ago, if it had been felt necessary to give Congress a power it did not then have, the power would have been created by a formal amendment to the Constitution, as was done for Prohibition. But since the time of the New Deal Amendments we have come to rely on the quick fix of legal fictions instead, legal fictions to a point where they tempt you to turn them into jokes.

Suppose somebody's dog habitually chases deer across a state line. Hunting deer, like duck hunting, supports a large industry, shipping millions of dollars worth of arms and ammunition across state lines, so obviously commerce is affected, and this and similar dogs may be regulated by Congress.

Or, your mother bakes a homemade cake. But she is not alone. Tens of millions of mothers bake homemade cakes and thereby each substantially affects interstate commerce in cakes, like the farmer who grew wheat for home consumption (*Wickard v. Filburn*). Congress may therefore regulate your mother's cake baking. First thing she needs is a permit.

In a recent case the Court held that the Corps of Engineers exceeded its authority under the Clean Water Act when the Corps claimed jurisdiction, on the basis of the "Migratory Bird Rule," over abandoned sand and gravel pits which were intended to be used for the disposal of solid waste materials by a local agency. (*Solid Waste Agency of Northern Cook County v. US Army Corps of Engineers* [decided January 9, 2001] 2001 WL 15333 [U.S.].) (References are to www.westlaw.com.)

The Court said:

In order to rule for [the Corps]..., we would have to hold that the jurisdiction of the Corps extends to ponds that are not adjacent to open water. But we conclude that the text of the statute will not allow this [2001 WL 15333 at *5].

We cannot agree that Congress' separate definitional use of the phrase "waters of the United States" constitutes a basis for reading the term "navigable waters" out of the statute [2001 WL 15333 at *6]).

We hold that [the Corps' regulation], as clarified and applied to [the local agency's] balefill site pursuant to the "Migratory Bird Rule" ... exceeds the authority granted to [the Corps] under the [Clean Water Act] [2001 WL 15333 at *8].

By the Court's well settled doctrine this holding made it unnecessary to consider the question of Congress' power under the Commerce Clause. But the Court gave a hint to Congress:

Twice in the past six years we have reaffirmed the proposition that the grant of authority to Congress under the Commerce Clause, though broad, is not unlimited [2001 WL 15333 at *7].

Yet the Court's decision was 5 to 4. The vote of only one justice stands between us and a Congress of unlimited powers.

Our waters needed cleaning, and are much cleaner today. But to achieve this, Congress has given the Constitution a body blow. Between 1948 and 1972, it seems there should have been time to work up a formal environmental powers amendment to the Constitution.

Chapter VIII

Endangered Species

To protect endangered species Congress used the "affecting commerce" legal fiction of the New Deal Commerce Clause Amendments to regulate behavior of people on their private lands in purely local matters. Disturb a hole in your backyard which belongs to an endangered species of rodent and you have committed a federal crime.

Congress legislated for the protection of wildlife as early as the Lacey Act of 1900 (31 Stat. 187; 16 USCA Sections 667[e] and 701. See *TVA v. Hill* [1978] 437 US 153, 57 L Ed 2d 117, at p. 134, 98 S Ct 2297). For the Lacey Act, Congress relied on the Commerce Clause. The Lacey Act prohibited the shipment in interstate commerce of fish and wildlife taken in violation of national, state, or foreign law. This type of clearly commerce-based protection was continued through various enactments, for example the Endangered Species Act of 1969 (83 Stat. 275), and is still in force in the currently applicable law, the Endangered Species Act of 1973 (87 Stat. 884, 16 USCA Section 1538 [a][1][A],[E]).

For other wildlife protection laws, Congress relied on its power to regulate federal lands, and also on the Commerce Clause.

Congress' power to "make all needful rules and regulations respecting the territory or other property belonging to the United States" (Constitution, Article IV, Section 3, Clause 2) was used to direct the federal agencies which administer the public lands to preserve endangered and threatened species "insofar as is practicable and consistent with" the primary mission of the respective agency (see, for example, the Endangered Species Act of 1966, 80 Stat. 926, Section 1[b]).

By the Endangered Species Act of 1973 (87 Stat. 884, 16 USCA Section 1531, et seq.) Congress went far beyond any of its previous enactments. The Supreme Court described the act as the most comprehensive legislation for the preservation of endangered species ever enacted by any nation ... Whereas predecessor statutes enacted in 1966 and 1969 had not contained any sweeping prohibition against the taking of endangered species except on federal lands ... the 1973 Act applied to all land in the United States and to the Nation's territorial seas ... among its central purposes is to provide a means whereby the ecosystems upon which endangered and threatened species depend may be conserved [*Babbitt v. Sweet Home Chapter of Communities for a Great Oregon* (1995) 515 US 687, 132 L Ed 2d 597, at p. 611, 115 S Ct 2407; internal quotation marks omitted].

Let this sink in for a moment: applied to *all* land in the United States.

Congress' constitutional power to regulate *federal* lands is clear, but where has Congress been given power by the Constitution to make laws regarding *all land* in the United States? There is no provision in the text of the Constitution giving Congress power over *all land* or *all waters* in the United States. So the power must be found, if it can be found, in some other power given to Congress.

Here we go again. Congress has power to regulate commerce. Commerce takes place on land (at least some of it), therefore Congress has power to regulate everything and anything on all land, public or private, within the United States. And pursuant to this "power" Congress made it

unlawful for any person subject to the jurisdiction of the United States to ... take any [endangered] species within the United States [16 USCA Section 1538(a)(1)(B); under certain circumstances a person may receive a permit and there are some hardship exemptions].

There is no pretense of a connection with interstate commerce in the text of this law. You take the species, without a permit, in your backyard, and you have committed a federal crime.

The end of the Endangered Species Act, to protect ecosystems and species, is undoubtedly desirable. But does that end justify the means? Does it justify the exercise of a power Congress was not given by the Constitution?

Besides the commerce power, there is in the Act a hint at the treaty power as a constitutional basis for enacting the Endangered Species Act:

The United States has pledged itself as a sovereign state in the international community to conserve to the extent practicable the various species of fish or wildlife and plants facing extinction, pursuant to—

(A) migratory bird treaties with Canada and Mexico [16 USCA Section 1531(a)(4); there follows a list of existing treaties].

Without determining whether the various treaties *require* the United States to enact a law making it a federal crime to "take" an endangered species in your backyard, there is the obvious question: could the president, with the agreement of "two-thirds of the Senators present" (Constitution, Article II, Section 2, Clause 2) amend the Constitution, so as to give Congress, by a treaty, a power the Constitution has not given to Congress?

For example, suppose 51 senators (a majority of the Senate must be present, to do business—Article I, Section 5, Clause 1) are in the chamber when the treaty comes up for "advice and consent." If 34 senators agree, the treaty becomes effective and suddenly Congress has a new power not previously given by the Constitution?

As citizens, when we read our contract among ourselves, the Constitution, we would best read it the way the Founders meant it to be read: "the words are to be taken in their natural and obvious sense, and not in a sense unreasonably restricted or enlarged" (Justice Story in *Martin v. Hunter's Lessee* [1816] 1 Wheat. 304; Kurland, Vol. 4, p. 305, No. 65).

Article V of the Constitution requires "two-thirds of both houses" of Congress to propose an amendment, and three-fourths of the state legislatures to make it effective. There is not a word about amendment of the Constitution by treaty in Article V.

Article II, Section 2, Clause 2, says that the President "shall have Power, by and with the Advice and Consent of the Senate, to make Treaties, provided two thirds of the Senators present concur."

If you give the words of Article V and Article II their natural and obvious meaning, then you must conclude that the treaty power was not intended to give the president and 34 senators the power to give to Congress a power *not given* by the Constitution, or, for that matter, to take away from Congress powers *given* by the Constitution.

So the wildlife treaties cannot justify the power exercised by Congress in the Endangered Species Act, namely, to make it a crime for you to "take," without a permit, an endangered species in your backyard.

Thus only the New Deal Commerce Clause legal fiction remains to account for Congress' power to create the crime of "taking endangered species."

This "power" is reaching even farther than appears at first glance. It is unlawful to "take" an endangered species. In today's plain English to "take" has many meanings. But among the first five given by the *Random House Webster's College Dictionary* (1997) is the meaning Congress obviously had in mind: "to catch or get (fish, game, etc.) esp. by killing." Congress defined this meaning of "take" in more detail: "The term 'take' means to harass, harm, pursue, hunt, shoot, wound, kill, trap, capture, or collect, or to attempt to engage in any such conduct" (16 USCA Section 1532 [19]).

In addition to this expansive definition, Congress gave the secretary of the interior power to make regulations to interpret the act. The secretary issued a regulation which further "defines" the word "harm" as it occurs in the section just quoted:

> *Harm* in the definition of "take" in the Act means an act which actually kills or injures wildlife. Such act may include significant habitat modification or degradation where it actually kills or injures wildlife by significantly impairing essential behavioral patterns, including breeding, feeding or sheltering [50 CFR Section 17.3 (1994). See *Babbitt v. Sweet Home Chapter of Communities for a Great Oregon* (1995) 515 US 687, 132 L Ed 2d 597, at p. 607, 115 S Ct 2407].

There you have it. Congress prohibits taking an endangered species on any land in the United States, including your backyard, and then lets the secretary stretch the law even farther, so that if an endangered rodent has its hole in your backyard, you can't even touch the hole, let alone the rodent, because the rodent needs the hole for "breeding ... or sheltering."

It is a worthy goal to preserve endangered species, but where in our contract among ourselves, the Constitution, have we given Congress such power?

The secretary's expansion of the meaning of "take" was attacked in the *Babbitt v. Sweet Home* case (see above), as going beyond what Congress had meant by using the words "take" and "harm."

The United States Supreme Court upheld the secretary's action. "Congress' *intent* to provide comprehensive protection for endangered and threatened species supports the permissibility of the Secretary's 'harm' regulation" (132 L Ed 2d at p. 612; emphasis added).

What Congress wanted to do (intent) decided the matter. The crucial question of where the Constitution gives Congress the power to regulate wildlife on "all land in the United States" in the first place, was not raised in the case. Apparently the New Deal Amendments' legal fiction that you regulate commerce when you regulate the habitat of a kangaroo rat was assumed as gospel. When the parties do not ask the question, the Court has no power to answer it. So the Court said nothing about that crucial question in the *Babbitt v. Sweet Home* case.

Three justices dissented. The dissenting opinion found that the statute did not authorize the secretary's definition of "harm":

> the legislation at issue here (1) forbade the hunting and killing of endangered animals, and (2) provided federal lands and federal funds *for the acquisition of private lands*, to preserve the habitat of endangered animals. The Court's holding that the hunting and killing prohibition incidentally preserves habitat on private land imposes unfairness to the point of financial ruin— not just upon the rich, but upon the simplest farmer who finds his land conscripted to national zoological use [132 L Ed 2d, at p. 621].

But the dissent did not discuss the crucial question, apparently because it had not been raised in the case.

The crucial question came up in the lower federal courts, and was decided in favor of the legal fiction of the New Deal Amendment.

In *National Association of Home Builders v. Babbitt* (1997) 130 F 3d 1041, the question was whether Congress had the constitutional power to regulate the "Delhi Sands Flower-Loving Fly, which lives only in the 'Delhi series' soils in southwestern San Bernardino County and northwestern Riverside County, California" (130 F 3d at p. 1043). The homebuilders' association argued that

> the federal government does not have the authority to regulate the use of non-federal lands in order to protect the Fly, which is found only within a single state ... they claim[ed] that the Constitution of the United States does not grant the federal government the authority to regulate wildlife, nor does it authorize federal regulation of nonfederal [sic] lands [130 F 3d, at p. 1045; internal quotation marks omitted].

If you look at the plain words of the Constitution, this is true. No such powers are given. You can create such powers for Congress only with the "affecting commerce" legal fiction of the New Deal Commerce Clause which we have met so often.

The court of appeals, by two judges, said that prohibiting change in the habitat of the Delhi Sands Flower-Loving Fly "constitutes a valid exercise of the Congress's authority to regulate interstate commerce under the Commerce Clause" (130 F 3d, at p. 1057).The two judges agreed the exercise of the power was constitutional, but couldn't agree on exactly how the fly substantially affected commerce.

The dissenting judge looked at the case from a common sense point of view. Here's how he stated the facts of the case:

> This case concerns the efforts of San Bernardino County, California ... to construct a hospital ... for its citizens.... Unfortunately those efforts discomfit an insect—the Delhi Sands Flower-Loving Fly ... there are fewer than 300 breeding individuals of this species, all located within forty square miles in Southern California.... In 1982, the County began considering construction of a $470 million "state-of-the-art," "earthquake-proof" hospital complex. The day before ground breaking ... the US Fish and Wildlife Service ... added the fly to the endangered species list and notified the County that construction of the hospital, on County land using County funds, would harm a colony of six to eight flies and would therefore violate federal law.... County officials were forced to move the hospital complex 250 feet northward and to set aside 8 acres of land for the fly ... costing county taxpayers around $3.5 million.... The Service also imposed a variety of other stringent requirements, including preservation of a flight corridor for the insect, which today prevents improvements to a traffic intersection necessary to allow emergency access.... At one point, the Service threatened to require shutting down the eight-lane San Bernardino Freeway ... for two months every year. (I am not making this up.) It did later drop this demand [130 F 3d, at p. 1060].

Next the dissenting judge described the law and the regulation, as they appear on the books, and raised the crucial question:

> we may take it as a given that the statute forbidding the taking of endangered species can be used, provided it passes constitutional muster, to prevent counties and their citizens from building hospitals or from driving to those hospitals by routes in which the bugs smashed upon their windshields might turn out to include the Delhi Sands Flower-Loving Fly or some other species of rare insect. That leaves the question for today as: by what constitutional justification does the federal government purport to regulate local activities that might disturb a local fly?... Can Congress under the Interstate Commerce Clause regulate the killing of flies, which is not commerce, in southern California, which is not interstate [130 F 3d, at p. 1061]?

The dissenting judge questioned the New Deal Commerce Clause legal fiction directly:

> So wide-ranging has been the application of the Clause as to prompt one writer to wonder why anyone would make the mistake of calling it the Commerce Clause instead of the "hey-you-can-do-whatever-you-feel-like clause" [130 F 3d, at p. 1061; internal quotation marks omitted].

The dissenting judge then pointed out that the U.S. Supreme Court, in the 1995 *Lopez* case (gun possession near a school) had made clear the limits of the Commerce Clause:

> (1) Congress may regulate the use of the channels of interstate commerce; (2) Congress is empowered to regulate and protect the instrumentalities of interstate commerce, or persons or things in interstate commerce, even though the threat may come only from intrastate activities; (3) Congress' commerce authority includes the power to regulate those activities having a substantial relation to interstate commerce [130 F 3d, at p. 1062; internal quotation marks omitted].

Judge Number 1, Judge Number 2, and the dissenting judge all agreed that category (2) did not apply. The dissenting judge and Judge Number 2 agreed that category (1) did not apply.

Judge Number 1 said that category (1), the channels of commerce, did apply. She argued that

> the prohibition against takings of endangered species is analogous to the prohibition against transfer and possession of machine guns (including purely intrastate possession).... [which is] a regulation of the use of the channels of interstate commerce because by regulating the market in machineguns, including regulating intrastate machinegun possession, Congress has effectively regulated the interstate traffic in machineguns....
>
> ...it is necessary to regulate possession of machine guns in order to regulate the interstate traffic in machineguns because it is impossible to sell machineguns in interstate commerce without first possessing them. Similarly, the prohibition on "taking" endangered species [can be upheld as a regulation of the use of the channels of interstate commerce] because one of the most effective ways to prevent traffic in endangered species is to secure the habitat of the species from predatory invasion and destruction [130 F 3d, at p. 1047; internal quotation marks omitted].

Do you see any similarity between regulating the possession of machine guns and protecting species' habitat? Wouldn't the proper analogy to protecting the fly in its habitat, be protecting the machine gun manufacturer in his habitat, the factory? The county did neither wish to "possess" nor to "transfer" any of the flies. So where's the analogy to "possessing" machine guns that might travel through interstate commerce? The fly was not going to be shipped in interstate commerce.

Moreover, the County did not "take" any of the flies in any real sense. It is a legal fiction that you "take" a fly when you disturb its habitat. Nobody wanted to buy or sell any of the flies in interstate commerce, or any other commerce.

Judge Number 1 also relied on "the authority of Congress to keep the channels of interstate commerce free from immoral or injurious uses." She said

> in this case Congress used this authority to prevent the eradication of an endangered species by a hospital that is presumably being constructed using materials and people from outside the state and which will attract employees, patients and students from both inside and outside the state. Thus, like regulations preventing racial discrimination or labor exploitation, regulations preventing the taking of endangered species prohibit interstate actors from using the channels of interstate commerce to promote or spread evil, whether of a physical, moral, or economic nature [130 F 3d, at p. 1048; internal quotation marks omitted].

The days when a hospital was a good thing, that couldn't hurt a fly, so to speak, are gone. Hospitals are now "interstate actors" that spread physical or moral evil, unless a watchful Congress steps in to prevent it.

The dissenting judge showed how the *channels of commerce* argument puts the Constitution on its head:

> [The] Judge ... seems to be trying to extend Congress' power over the channels of commerce to allow direct federal regulation of any local effects caused by any activity using those channels of commerce. She focuses not on the fly in the channels of commerce, but everything else moving in the channels of commerce that may affect the fly... [130 F 3d, at p. 1063].

Commerce may affect the fly—but the fly does not affect Commerce. If the fly does not affect commerce, how can Congress regulate it on the ground that it is "affecting commerce?"

Judge Number 1 and Judge Number 2 had different theories of how the fly *substantially affects* interstate commerce: "biodiversity" and "the interconnectedness of species and ecosystems." As to the "biodiversity" argument, the dissenting judge commented:

Under this rationale, she argues that the extinction of a species, and the concomitant diminution of the pool of wild species, "has a substantial effect on interstate commerce by diminishing a natural resource that could otherwise be used for present and future commercial purposes."

The dissenting judge asked:

because of some undetermined and indeed undeterminable possibility that the fly might produce something at some undefined and undetermined future time which might have some undefined and undeterminable medical value, which in turn might affect interstate commerce at that imagined future point, Congress can today regulate anything which might advance the pace at which the endangered species becomes extinct [130 F 3d at p. 1064].

As to the "interconnectedness" argument, the dissenting judge said:

As I understand her rationale, it depends on the interconnectedness of species and ecosystems which she deems sufficient for us to conclude that the extinction of one species affects others and their ecosystems and that the protection of a purely intrastate species ... will therefore substantially affect land and objects that are involved in interstate commerce....

...the Commerce Clause empowers Congress to "regulate commerce" not "ecosystems." ... There is no showing, but only the rankest of speculation, that a reduction or even complete destruction of the viability of the Delhi Sands Flower-Loving Fly will in fact affect land and objects that are involved in interstate commerce ... let alone do so substantially ... nor has my colleague supplied a reason why this basis of regulation would apply to the preservation of a species any more than [to] any other act potentially affecting the continued and stable existence of any other item of a purely intrastate nature upon which one might rest a speculation that its loss or change could somehow affect some other object, land, or otherwise, that might be involved in interstate commerce [130 F 3d, at p. 1065].

The dissenting judge concluded his opinion as follows:

In the end, attempts to regulate the killing of a fly under the Commerce Clause fail because there is certainly no interstate commerce in the Delhi Sands Flower-Loving Fly. The whole effort to employ a clause that empowers Congress to regulate commerce in order to serve a perhaps worthy but wholly non-commercial goal of preserving an endangered fly calls to mind the thoughts of the first great commentator on the Constitution, Justice Joseph Story. Story considered the then current question of whether the constitutional authority to regulate commerce could be applied to the perhaps worthy "purpose of encouraging and protecting domestic manufactures." He declared, "If this were admitted, the enumeration of the powers of congress would be wholly unnecessary and nugatory. Agriculture, colonies, capital, machinery, the wages of labour, the profits of stock, the rents of land, the punctual performance of contracts, and the diffusion of knowledge would all be within the scope of the power; for all of them bear an intimate relation to commerce. The result would be, that the powers of congress would embrace the widest extent of legislative functions, to the utter demolition of all constitutional boundaries between the state and national governments.... The power to regulate manufactures is no more confided to congress, than the power to interfere with the systems of education, the poor laws, or the road laws of the states" [130 F 3d, at p. 1067].

We have met with Justice Story in Chapter I. When I read the Delhi Sands Fly case, I was pleased to see that Justice Story, and the Old Constitution, are remembered by at least some of our judges.

I have quoted at length from the Delhi Sands Fly case to show you the tortured and convoluted reasoning used by our judges to squeeze nearly every subject on which Congress has legislated under the cover of the Commerce Clause.

It is a bad joke, like the old high school joke about the Frenchman visiting New York City. His hosts show him the sights, the Battery, the Statue of Liberty, the Brooklyn Bridge, the Empire State Building, the Cloisters, and so on. At the first sight, they ask him, does this remind him of anything? He says, it reminds me of the sinuous lines of a voluptuous woman. At every other sight, same question, same answer. Finally they ask him—Why? He says, *Everything* reminds me of...

Here's Congress for you—*Everything* reminds them of—*Commerce.* This really is a bad joke, but it's true.

The long quotes from the Fly Case show something else. We still have judges with common sense, though they appear to be the minority. But before we start blaming the judiciary, let us remember that it was President Franklin Roosevelt, backed by the majority of Congress, backed by the majority of the people, who forced the Supreme Court, and with it the entire judiciary, into this game of legal fictions. In the *Schechter Poultry, Carter Coal,* and *Butler* cases (see Chapter I), the Supreme Court held on to the plain meaning of the Constitution: "Commerce" means commerce, not agriculture and not manufacturing, and "among the several states" does not mean within one state only. But the pressure of public opinion forced the Court to flee into the legal fiction, hatched by Congress, that "commerce" includes matters "affecting commerce." This opened the floodgate of legal fictions leading to where disturbing a local fly's habitat by building a hospital means "taking" the fly, and "taking" it "substantially affects" commerce among the several states, because some of the building materials for the hospital may have crossed state lines.

Our New Deal chickens are coming home to roost. We have become so used to the quick fix of legal fictions that we have ceased amending the Constitution to give Congress new powers when we believe it to be necessary. Instead, we just let Congress give these powers, and then some, to itself by evermore expanding the legal fiction of "affecting commerce."

The Fly Case was presented for review to the United States Supreme Court, but the Court declined, without opinion, to review the case. (*National Association of Homebuilders v. Babbitt* [June 22, 1998] 524 US n.a., 141 L Ed 2d 712, 118 S Ct n.a.)

In the 1995 *Lopez* case, the Court had stated the limits of the Commerce Clause. By a common sense reading, the Fly Case disregarded these limits. Why did the Court not step in to correct this error? We can only speculate. Did the Court feel itself bound, because in the *Sweet Home* case it had upheld the regulation which later in the Fly Case was read to mean that you "take" a fly when you disturb its habitat? Did the Court feel that it was too late to tell Congress, 25 years after the enactment of the Endangered Species Act, that in some parts of the act Congress had gone beyond its powers? Did the Court want to avoid getting clobbered, New Deal style, by the apparently vast and impatient public support for conservation (though this was perhaps not really a majority, but a well-organized minority supported by a majority of the media)?

Whatever the cause, the Court did not review the Delhi Sands Fly case. So the present state of judicial precedent is that the Commerce Clause has limits, as shown in the *Lopez* case (gun possession near school), but that these limits appear to have no force when it comes to endangered species (Delhi Sands Fly case).

You should not blame the courts for this muddled state of affairs. The cause is the New Deal Commerce Clause legal fiction, "affecting commerce," which was the particular invention of Congress.

Nor should you blame the "faceless bureaucrats." The civil servants who administer the law through the departments and agencies of the federal government are doing what Congress told them to do. Congress told them to go and protect the environment and the wildlife. Do it on *all land* in the United States and protect *the waters* of the United States, and make broad regulations to do all this. So they do. It is not for the civil servants to say: this law is unconstitutional.

The blame lies squarely with Congress.

Chapter IX

The Arts

Congress began to provide taxpayer money for the arts with the National Foundation on the Arts ... Act of 1965 (79 Stat. 895). By this act, the National Endowment for the Arts was set up to administer grants-in-aid to the states, to private groups, and to private individuals. The 1965 statute was amended several times and is now part of the *United States Code* (20 USCA Section 951, et seq.).

Where does the Constitution provide that Congress should spend taxpayer money on the fine arts?

There is one reference in the Constitution to the "arts," but it is to the "useful arts," which Congress is to promote by the grant of patents and copyrights for limited periods. The records of the convention for the drafting of the Constitution contain a proposal "To establish seminaries for the promotion of literature and the arts and sciences" (Kurland, Vol. 3, p. 40, No. 6 [1787], Journal, 18 Aug., Records of the Federal Convention).

That same Journal entry contains additional proposals, including provisions for patents and copyrights. But all of these proposals were dropped. Only the provision that is now Article I, Section 8, Clause 8, of the Constitution was adopted and became part of the powers granted to Congress:

> To promote the progress of science and useful arts by securing for limited times to Authors and Inventors the exclusive right to their respective writings and discoveries [Kurland, Vol. 3, p. 40, No. 6 (1787), Journal, 5 Sept., Records of the Federal Convention: the committee agreed to this version].

The Founders apparently had no intention to set up Congress as a patron of the fine arts. Patents for the "useful arts" was the limit. So where does Congress get the power to spend taxpayer money on the fine arts?

In the declaration of findings and purposes of the statute Congress does not say from which part of the Constitution it draws this power (20 USCA Section 951). Since Congress spends taxpayer money on the arts, we can only assume that it is the ubiquitous power "To ... collect Taxes ... to ... provide for the common Defence and general Welfare of the United States" known as the Spending Power (Article I, Section 8, Clause 1). We meet again with the problem, already encountered in the context of education and housing: Is the "general Welfare" the welfare of *all* Americans, or is it the sum total of individual "welfares" in the country, which sum is increased, if any one individual or group receives more than they previously had. This, of course, does not count the decrease inflicted on the taxpayer who does not receive any benefit.

Congress stated (20 USCA Section 951): "(1) The arts and the humanities belong to all the people of the United States." Do they "belong" even to people who do not want them? Does the Constitution give Congress the power to spend people's money to make them care about the fine arts?

> (2) The encouragement and support of national progress and scholarship in the humanities and the arts, while primarily a matter for private and local initiative, are also appropriate matters of concern to the Federal Government.

Why are the fine arts "appropriate matters" for federal concern, when the Constitution speaks only of promoting "science and the useful arts?"

> (3) An advanced civilization must not limit its efforts to science and technology alone, but must give full value and support to the other great branches of scholarly and cultural activity in order to achieve a better understanding of the past, a better analysis of the present, and a better view of the future.
>
> (4) Democracy demands wisdom and vision in its citizens. It must therefore foster and support a form of education, and access to the arts and the humanities, designed to make people of all backgrounds and wherever located masters of their technology and not its unthinking servants.

That may be true, but where does the Constitution say that the national government "must" see to that? As we have seen, the Founders rejected this role for the national government, and told it to promote "science and the useful arts" (i.e., science and technology) instead. Why would

Congress suddenly have the power to decide that not enough is being done for the arts in our universities and other institutions?

Where does the Constitution say that Congress is to take our tax money to teach us how to gain wisdom and vision?

> (5) It is necessary and appropriate for the Federal Government to complement, assist, and add to programs for the advancement of the humanities and the arts by local, state, regional, and private agencies and their organizations.... Public funds provided by the Federal Government must ultimately serve public purposes the Congress defines.
>
> (6) The arts and the humanities reflect the high place accorded by the American people to the nation's rich cultural heritage and to the fostering of mutual respect for the diverse beliefs and values of all persons and groups.
>
> (7) The practice of art and the study of the humanities require constant dedication and devotion. While no government can call a great artist or scholar into existence, it is necessary and appropriate for the Federal Government to help create and sustain not only a climate of encouraging freedom of thought, imagination and inquiry but also the material conditions facilitating the release of this creative talent.
>
> (8) The world leadership which has come to the United States cannot rest solely upon superior power, wealth and technology, but must be solidly founded upon worldwide respect and admiration for the Nation's high qualities as a leader in the realm of ideas and the spirit.
>
> (9) Americans should receive in school, background and preparation in the arts and humanities to enable them to recognize and appreciate the aesthetic dimensions of our lives, the diversity of excellence that comprises our cultural heritage, and artistic and scholarly expression.

Now it has become not only "appropriate," but even "necessary," that Congress should spend your tax money to have somebody teach you the "values" of "diversity," and so forth! You better believe that diversity and multiculturalism are good for you—Congress said so.

> (10) It is vital to a democracy to honor and preserve its multicultural artistic heritage as well as support new ideas, and therefore it is essential to provide financial assistance to its artists and the organizations that support their work.
>
> (11) To fulfill its educational mission, achieve an orderly continuation of free society, and provide models of excellence to the American people, the Federal Government must transmit the achievement and values of civilization from the past via the present to the future, and make widely available the greatest achievements of art.

The longer Congress talks, the more urgent becomes the need to spend taxpayers' money. Here Congress tells you that it is not only "necessary" but "vital" and "essential" for you to provide financial assistance with your tax money to "artists" and to organizations that support multicultural artistic activities, and the federal government has an "educational mission" to teach you about "the greatest achievements of art." All the Constitution tells Congress is to promote "science and the useful arts" by patents and copyrights. There's nothing in it about "educational missions," or a ministry of propaganda.

> (12) In order to implement these findings and purposes, it is desirable to establish a National Foundation of the Arts and the Humanities.

Do you agree that it is "desirable" to set up another federal bureaucracy, and to pay it $21,200,000 (in fiscal 1991) to distribute $125,800,000 (in fiscal 1991) (20 USCA Section 960 [a], [c]) to state agencies, private organizations, and "individuals of exceptional talent engaged in or concerned with the arts" (20 USCA Section 954[c])?

Presumably all this is to be defended as being for the "general Welfare." But it is clear that this program is *not* for the "general Welfare" in the sense of the welfare of *all* Americans. An art exhibition in New York or an amateur theatrical in Dubuque are of decidedly local benefit, unless you want to argue that all Americans could go to New York or Dubuque to see the show.

So if it is "general Welfare," it would have to be the "sum of goodness" general welfare we have encountered in the context of housing (Chapter IV) and of education (Chapter III). Some "artists," theatres and local symphonies are better off after receiving a grant. Therefore the sum of "better off" persons in the country has increased. Therefore the "general Welfare" of the country has increased. Therefore the grants are for the "general Welfare." Are you convinced?

In the context of the arts, there is an additional factor that is not present in federal spending on housing and the like. By spending for the arts the federal government forces some citizens to contribute money for the expression of ideas which they dislike or even hate.

Speaking in 1779 about forced contributions to the church established by the state of Virginia, Thomas Jefferson said:

to compel a man to furnish contributions of money for the propaga-
tion of opinions which he disbelieves and abhors, is sinful and tyran-
nical....
... the opinions of men are not the subject of civil government,
nor under its jurisdiction [Kurland, Vol. 5, p. 77, No. 37, Thomas
Jefferson, A Bill For Establishing Religious Freedom, 12 June 1779].

These words are as true in the context of the "arts" as they were in the
context of religion. Western art has been in the service of the church
for a thousand years or more. It illustrated the gospels for the illiterate
multitude. It broke loose from the church only a few hundred years ago,
turning to non-religious subjects. Of late, some art has turned around
to attack religion. What business does Congress have to favor one side
of the argument, or the other, with taxpayer money?

Whether attacking religion, or otherwise offending citizens' sense
of decency, or simply supporting activity a great many of the citizens
do not care about and would not buy in the market, Congress' spending of taxpayer money to "educate" taxpayers for their own good seems
singularly inappropriate.

The Supreme Court has recently sketched the whole picture:

Since 1965, the NEA [National Endowment for the Arts] has distributed over three billion dollars in grants to individuals and organizations, funding that has served as a catalyst for increased state,
corporate, and foundation support for the arts....
... By far the largest portion of the grants distributed in fiscal
year 1998 were awarded directly to state arts agencies. In the remain-
ing categories, the most substantial grants were allocated to symphony
orchestras, fine arts museums, dance theater foundations, and opera
associations....
... Throughout the NEA's history, only a handful of the agency's
roughly 100,000 awards have generated formal complaints about mis-
applied funds or abuse of the public's trust. Two provocative works,
however, prompted public controversy in 1989 and led to congressional revaluation of the NEA's funding priorities and efforts to
increase oversight of its grant-making procedures. The Institute of
Contemporary Art at the University of Pennsylvania had used $30,000
of a visual arts grant it received from the NEA to fund a 1989 retro-
spective of photographer Robert Mapplethorpe's work. The exhibit,
entitled *The Perfect Moment*, included homoerotic photographs that
several members of Congress condemned as pornographic...
Members also denounced artist Andres Serrano's work *Piss
Christ*, a photograph of a crucifix immersed in urine.... Serrano had
been awarded a $15,000 grant from the Southeast Center for the

Contemporary Arts, an organization that received NEA support [*National Endowment for the Arts v. Finley* (1998) 524 US 569, 141 L Ed 2d 500, at p. 507–508, 118 S Ct 2168].

The amounts involved are small, by federal standards, but the principle is large. Taxpayers are forced to contribute to the expression of opinions which they abhor.

Reliably enough, some "artists" came to see federal arts money as an entitlement and sued the NEA when they did not receive any. In the *Finley* case,

> the *oeuvres d'art* for which the four individual plaintiffs in this case sought funding have been described as follows:
> Finley's controversial show, "We Keep Our Victims Ready," contains three segments. In the second segment, Finley visually recounts a sexual assault by stripping to the waist and smearing chocolate on her breasts and by using profanity to describe the assault. Holly Hughes monologue, "World Without End," is a somewhat graphic recollection of the artist's realization of her lesbianism and reminiscence of her mother's sexuality. John Fleck, in his stage performance, "Blessed Are All The Little Fishes," confronts alcoholism and Catholicism. During the course of the performance, Fleck appears dressed as a mermaid, urinates on the stage and creates an altar out of a toilet bowl by putting a photograph of Jesus Christ on the lid. Tim Miller derives his performance "Some Golden States" from childhood experiences, from his life as a homosexual, and from the constant threat of AIDS. Miller uses vegetables in his performances to represent sexual symbols [*NEA v. Finley* 141 L Ed 2d, at p. 521–522, n. 2; internal quotation marks omitted].

When the NEA turned their application down, they argued in court that by turning down their application for taxpayers' money, the government was suppressing their free expression of ideas. By that reasoning the organizers of "The Ecstatic," a recent pro-drug exhibition in New York, also would have been entitled to taxpayers' money so as not to suppress their expression of ideas (*The Wall Street Journal*, September 17, 1999, "Soros Says Yes to Pro-Drug Art Exhibition").

This argument turns the First Amendment on its head. Instead of "Congress shall make no law ... abridging the freedom of speech," they want the First Amendment to read: Congress shall make laws to pay everybody for expressing their ideas.

The Court upheld the NEA's decision to deny the Finley group's application. The Court's opinion is somewhat murky, but a concurring opinion, supported by two justices, stated the matter clearly:

> Those who wish to create indecent and disrespectful art are as unconstrained now as they were before the enactment of this statute. *Avant-garde artistes* such as respondents remain entirely free to *épater les bourgeois* [to shock "conventional" people]; they are merely deprived of the additional satisfaction of having the bourgeoisie taxed to pay for it. It is preposterous to equate the denial of a taxpayer subsidy with measures aimed at the suppression of dangerous ideas [*NEA v. Finley* 141 L Ed 2d, at p. 521–522; internal quotation marks omitted].

The important lesson of the *Finley* case is that Congress has no business in the first place to pay taxpayer money to artists, to art promotion groups, or to anybody else to "express" themselves or their "ideas." If Congress had stayed away from giving taxpayer money to the "arts," we would not have had the ludicrous spectacle of artists arguing in court that they are entitled to our money to express themselves however they like. They are free to do so at any time, but not on our money.

Despite the unctuous, vapid, self-aggrandizing sermon in Section 951 (20 USCA Section 951), Congress simply has no business to determine that "Americans should receive in school, background and preparation in the arts, and so on."

To repeat Jefferson's admonition: "the opinions of men are not the object of civil government." When Big Brother tells you should "appreciate the aesthetic dimension of [your] life and the diversity of excellence that comprises our cultural heritage" he is dictating your opinion.

But it might be that some citizens believe that getting their opinion dictated by Big Brother contributes to the "general Welfare." It will be up to a majority of the citizens in each State to resolve this question.

Chapter X

Prisons

The Supreme Court has, in effect, amended the Eighth, Thirteenth and Fourteenth Amendments to the United States Constitution. The new Eighth Amendment and the Due (process of) Law Clause of the Fourteenth Amendment have become what a dissenting justice has accurately described as The National Code of Prison Regulation.

Does the United States Constitution give to the federal courts any power over state prisons? There is no express provision for such a power. Is such a power implied in the provisions of the federal Constitution which relate to state criminal law and thus might have something to do with state prisons?

The Thirteenth Amendment says:

> Section 1. Neither slavery nor involuntary servitude, except as a punishment for crime whereof the party shall have been duly convicted, shall exist within the United States, or any place subject to their jurisdiction.

Taking the words of the amendment in "their natural and obvious sense, and not in a sense unreasonably restricted or enlarged" (Kurland, Vol. 4, p. 305, No. 65, Justice Story, in *Martin v. Hunter's Lessee* [1816]), it seems that if a person is being subjected to "involuntary servitude" in a state prison without having been "duly convicted," the federal courts could properly become involved, because involuntary servitude (absent a lawful conviction) shall not "exist within the United States." The amendment, taken in its natural and obvious sense, must give power to the federal courts to inquire whether the person in the state prison has been "duly convicted" of the crime in question. Otherwise involuntary servitude in violation of the amendment could "exist" in the United States. But there are no words in the amendment giving a power to the federal courts to determine how a person, after being "duly convicted," is to be treated during that person's "involuntary servitude."

The Fourteenth Amendment says:

> ...nor shall any State deprive any person of life, liberty, or property, without due process of law [Amendment XIV, Section 1].

The natural and obvious meaning of "due process of law" is the process or procedure by which the law is properly applied by the judge and the jury in a given case (See Introduction). Once due process has been properly followed, a state may, for example, deprive a person of the person's liberty.

"To deprive" means:

> 1. to remove or withhold something from the enjoyment or possession of (a person or persons): *to deprive a man of life.*

"Servitude" means:

> 1. slavery or bondage of any kind:...
> 2. compulsory service or labor as a punishment for criminals: penal servitude.
> [*The Random House Dictionary of the English Language,* Unabridged Edition, 1967.]

A person is deprived of liberty by being placed into involuntary servitude, as punishment for crime. Neither the Thirteenth nor the Fourteenth Amendment says anything about how the person is to be treated, once the person is deprived of liberty in accordance with due process of law, other than that he may be held in "involuntary servitude."

The Eighth Amendment says:

> Excessive bail shall not be required, nor excessive fines imposed, nor cruel and unusual punishments inflicted.

Bail relates to the proceedings before a person has been convicted. A fine is "imposed" by the judgment of a court, after conviction. All that remains to be done, after that, is to pay the fine.

When is the punishment of a term of involuntary servitude (which is to say, a prison term) "inflicted?"

In plain modern English "to inflict" means:

> 1. to lay on: *to inflict a dozen lashes.*
> 2. to impose as something that must be borne or suffered: *to inflict punishment.*

3. to impose (anything unwelcome): *the regime inflicted burdensome taxes on the people* [*The Random House Dictionary of the English Language*, Unabridged Edition, 1967].

Meaning No. 2. seems the natural and obvious meaning of "inflict," as the word is used in the Eighth Amendment. Punishment is "inflicted" when a court's judgment imposes a term of involuntary servitude on a defendant. What does "cruel" mean?

1. willfully and knowingly causing pain or distress to others.
2. enjoying the pain or distress of others.
3. causing or marked by great pain or distress.
4. rigid; stern; strict; unrelentingly severe [*The Random House Dictionary of the English Language*, Unabridged Edition, 1967].

When a government condemns a criminal to a term of involuntary servitude, it is done with the knowledge that this will cause distress to the criminal. In sense Number 1, therefore, *all punishment* is "cruel." Obviously the Eighth Amendment was not intended to prohibit all punishment. Punishment that is both, cruel *and* unusual must be what is forbidden.

"Unusual" means in plain English "not usual, common, or ordinary; uncommon in amount or degree; exceptional" (*The Random House Dictionary of the English Language*, Unabridged Edition, 1967).

A term of fifteen years of involuntary servitude (i.e., a 15 year prison term) would be "cruel and unusual" if imposed for the crime of "cheeking the police" (See *The Wind in the Willows*, Chapter 6) because that is not the usual punishment for that offense in this country. But the same term of involuntary servitude would not be "cruel and unusual," if imposed for a more serious offense.

Thus the Eighth Amendment, by the natural and obvious meaning of its words, does not prohibit "cruel" punishment that is usual (for example, the death penalty for murder), and it does not prohibit "unusual" punishment that is not cruel (for example, some unusual requirement of making restitution, or of community service). It prohibits punishment that is *both* cruel *and* unusual.

This is what we get when we read the words of the Constitution in their natural and obvious meaning in today's plain English.

Bail, fines, and punishment all relate to the court proceedings leading to conviction and judgment. Thus the Eighth Amendment is addressed to the courts, and, possibly, to the legislature, telling them what kind of sentences are prohibited by the Constitution.

Of course, if you pluck the words "nor cruel and unusual punishment" from their context, you can say that, standing alone, these words prohibit cruel and unusual punishment inflicted anywhere, by anybody, including prison guards, teachers, baseball umpires, parents, and so on. But in the Eighth Amendment to the Constitution these words do not stand alone. They stand in the context of criminal court proceedings.

How did the Founders understand the words of the Eighth Amendment?

These words came from the English Bill of Rights of 1689, which had been enacted by Parliament after the "glorious revolution" of 1688 in which King James II had been deprived of the Crown and forced to go abroad. "Glorious" to the English, because the revolution had been achieved without bloodshed. (G.M. Trevelyan, *History of England*, London: Longman, reprint 1952, Vol. 2, p. 270).

The English Bill of Rights says in Section 10:

> excessive bail ought not to be required, nor excessive fines imposed; nor cruel and unusual punishments inflicted (Kurland, Vol. 5, p. 369, No. 2, Bill of Rights, Sec. 10 [16 Dec. 1689]).

In the court of King's Bench, during the reign of James II, punishments had been inflicted by the judges that were without precedent, and therefore "unusual." For example, Titus Oates, a cleric who had given false testimony in prosecutions of Catholics, was sentenced to life imprisonment, to stand in the pillory every year on the dates about which he had committed perjury, to "be whipped from Aldgate to Newgate" on one day, and to "be whipped from Newgate to Tyburn, by the hands of the common hangman" two days later. On appeal, a minority in the House of Lords dissented on the ground

> that there is [sic] no precedents to warrant the punishment of whipping and committing to prison for life, for the crime of perjury....
> ...that the said judgments [are] contrary to law and ancient practice, and therefore erroneous and ought to be reversed. (Kurland, Vol. 5, p. 368–369, No. 1 [1685]).

The English Bill of Rights was directed against such abuses of judicial power.

After the Thirteen Colonies declared their independence, Section 10 of the English Declaration of Rights was adopted in many of the fundamental laws of the new states. Some of the states used exactly the same words (Kurland, Vol. 5, p. 373, No. 5, Virginia (1776), No. 7, Delaware (1776)].

Other states attacked the problem of cruel punishments directly, by substituting their own ideas about proper punishments for those of the English common law. The constitution of Pennsylvania provided in 1776:

> Sec. 29. Excessive bail shall not be exacted for bailable offenses: And all fines shall be moderate...
>
> Sec. 38. The penal laws as heretofore used shall be reformed by the legislature of this state, as soon as may be, and punishments made in some cases less sanguinary, and in general more proportionate to the crimes [Kurland, Vol. 5, p. 373, No. 8].

Similarly in 1778 Thomas Jefferson proposed to the Virginia legislature "A Bill For Proportioning Crimes And Punishments." Among its proportionate punishments were the following:

> Whosoever commiteth murder by poisoning shall suffer death by poison....
>
> Whosoever shall be guilty of Rape, Polygamy, or Sodomy with man or woman shall be punished, if a man, by castration, if a woman, by cutting thro' the cartilage of her nose a hole of one half inch diameter at the least....
>
> Whosoever on purpose ... shall maim another, or shall disfigure him ... shall be maimed or disfigured in like sort: or if that cannot be for want of the same part, then as nearly as may be in some other part of at least equal value and estimation in the opinion of a jury [Kurland, Vol. 5, p. 374-375, No. 10 (1778)].

As of 1792, the Delaware Constitution's equivalent of the Eighth Amendment provided that

> Excessive bail shall not be required, nor excessive fines imposed, nor cruel and unusual punishments inflicted; *and in the construction of jails a proper regard shall be had to the health of the prisoners.* (Del. Declaration of Rights, Art. I, Section XI [emphasis added].

[As quoted in *Helling v. McKinney* (1993) 509 US 25, 125 L Ed 2d 22, at p. 35, 113 S Ct 2475.]

The Supreme Court justice who quoted this provision in 1993 remarked: "when members of the founding generation wished to make prison conditions a matter of constitutional guarantee, they knew how to do so" (125 L Ed 2d, at p. 35).

After the United States Constitution had been adopted, the first Congress debated the proposed American Bill of Rights (which contained what are now the First through Tenth Amendments). Only brief discussion regarding "cruel and unusual punishment" has been reported. There were some objections to the phrase:

> Mr. SMITH, of South Carolina, objected to the words "nor cruel and unusual punishments"; the import of them being too indefinite.
> Mr. LIVERMORE.—The clause seems to express a great deal of humanity, on which account I have no objection to it; but as it seems to have no meaning in it, I do not think it necessary.... No cruel and unusual punishment is to be inflicted; it is sometimes necessary to hang a man, villains often deserve whipping, and perhaps having their ears cut off; but are we in future to be prevented from inflicting these punishments because they are cruel? If a more lenient way of correcting vice and deterring others from the commission of it could be invented, it would be very prudent in the Legislature to adopt it; but until we have some security that this will be done, we ought not to be restrained from making necessary laws by any declaration of this kind [Kurland, Vol. 5, p. 377, No. 14 (1789)].

Notwithstanding such objections, the Eighth Amendment was adopted. Its prohibition of cruel and unusual punishments was later described as showing "the sense of the whole community" against what Americans felt were the barbarous punishments of the English common law (Kurland, Vol. 5, p. 386, No. 19 [1824]).

In England the prohibition of such punishments was directed at the Crown, acting through the judges of King's Bench, but not against Parliament (Kurland, Vol. 5, p. 376, No. 11 [1788]). In America, the words were thought to limit the legislative power as well as the executive power. It was feared that Congress might invent "the most cruel and un-heard of punishments" (Kurland, Vol. 5, p. 376–377, Nos. 11, 12, 13 [1788]). There was, however, also concern about limiting Congress too strictly, so that it would not be able to devise new punishments, where traditional punishments had failed (Kurland, Vol. 5, p. 387, No. 21 [1829]; p. 377, No. 1 4 [1789]).

But the Founders did not adopt constitutional limitations on the manner in which Congress would regulate federal prisons, let alone on how the states would maintain their prisons. The Eighth Amendment was aimed only at limiting the powers of the federal government. One hundred and fifty six years went by before the Supreme Court even arguably considered the Eighth Amendment applicable to the states, by force of the Due Process of Law Clause of the Fourteenth Amendment (*Louisiana ex rel. Francis v. Resweber* [1947] 329 US 459, 91 L Ed 422, 67 S Ct 374).

During the 19th Century, even after the adoption of the Fourteenth Amendment in 1868, the Eighth Amendment was held to apply against the federal government only. The relatively few U.S. Supreme Court cases that arose during that period, the history of the amendment, and the treatment of its state constitution equivalents by some of the state courts, are described in *Weems v. United States* (1910) 217 US 349, 54 L Ed 793, at p. 799–802, 30 S Ct 544.

Weems had been a disbursing officer of the coast guard of the "United States Government of the Philippine Islands." He had falsified government records by showing 204 pesos and 408 pesos, respectively, as paid out to the employees at two lighthouses. Under the Philippine Code he was sentenced to fifteen years of imprisonment at hard and painful labor, all the time in chains connecting ankle and wrist, a fine of 4000 pesetas, loss of certain civil rights during the prison term, perpetual disqualification from voting or holding office and perpetual surveillance by the authorities after release from prison.

The United States Supreme Court held that, under the Bill of Rights, which had been made part of the law of the Philippines when the United States took over the Philippines, Weems' sentence was "cruel and unusual punishment." The Court said:

> Such penalties for such offenses amaze those who have formed their conception of the relation of a state to even its offending citizens from the practice of the American commonwealths, and believe that it is a precept of justice that punishment for crime should be graduated and proportioned to offense [217 US, at p. 366–367, 54 L Ed, at p. 798].

The Court held that the Eighth Amendment, originally directed against the barbarous punishments of the old English common law, applied also against any disproportionate punishment imposed by the United States government, including the territorial government of the Philippines:

> Time works changes, brings into existence new conditions and purposes. Therefore a principle, to be vital, must be capable of wider application than the mischief which gave it birth [217 US, at p. 373, 54 L Ed, at p. 801].

> The [Eighth Amendment to] the Constitution ... may be there-
> fore progressive, and is not fastened to the obsolete, but may acquire
> meaning as public opinion becomes enlightened by a humane justice.
> [217 US, at p. 378, 54 L Ed, at p. 803].

These principles were followed by the Court in this century.
But in time the Court progressed from interpreting the words of the
Eighth Amendment in the light of humane justice, to informally
amending the amendment, by applying it outside the scope set by its
words.

The words "bail ... required," "fines imposed," "punishments
inflicted," place the amendment into the context of criminal court proceedings. To apply the "cruel and unusual punishment" test to conditions in prisons which are not a part of the sentence imposed by a court,
you must tear the phrase from its context in the amendment. Then,
standing alone, the phrase can in plain English refer to any "punishment inflicted" by anybody, anywhere, including in a prison. But what
is meant by "punishment" as used in the Amendment?

In plain English "punishment" means

> 1. act of punishing. 2. fact of being punished, as for an offense or fault.
> 3. a penalty inflicted for an offense, fault, etc. 4. severe handling or
> treatment [*The Random House Dictionary of the English Language*,
> Unabridged Edition, 1967].

The natural and obvious meaning of "punishment" as used in the
Amendment, is Number 3, "a penalty inflicted for an offense." If the
penalty inflicted is imprisonment, then you would have to consider
every incident of prison life a separate "punishment," in order to apply
the test of "cruel and unusual" to that incident.

So to make the Eighth Amendment control conditions of prison
life, you first have to take the phrase "cruel and unusual punishment"
from its criminal court proceedings context in the amendment and secondly, shift the word "punishment" from the natural and obvious
meaning, number 3 to meaning number 4: "severe treatment." In effect,
the amendment then would say: "Excessive bail shall not be required,
nor excessive fines imposed, nor cruel and unusual punishments
inflicted," <u>nor imprisonment administered in a cruel and unusual man-
ner</u>.

The step from interpretation to informal amendment was taken in
Estelle v. Gamble (1976) 429 US 97, 50 L Ed 2d 251, 97 S Ct 285.

Gamble, a Texas convict, had been hurt by a bale of cotton falling on him while he was unloading a truck during a prison work assignment. He continued to work, but after four hours he became stiff and was granted a pass to the prison hospital. During the three months that followed, Gamble was seen by doctors 11 times, once by a nurse, and six times by a medical assistant. He received various medications, to control pain, muscle spasms, high blood pressure, and heart problems.

Thereafter, he brought a civil rights action in federal court, based on an alleged lack of diagnosis and treatment of his back injury.

Gamble did not challenge his sentence. He had been duly convicted and was then serving his time of involuntary servitude as punishment for crime. Yet he was permitted to sue in federal court, like a free citizen. He alleged a violation of constitutional rights, namely that not getting better diagnosis and treatment of his back injury than he had in fact received was the same as subjecting him to "cruel and unusual punishment" contrary to the Eighth Amendment, made applicable to the states by the Fourteenth Amendment.

What constitutional rights could he have, being properly in "involuntary servitude" as punishment for crime, as authorized by the Thirteenth Amendment? What happened to the Thirteenth Amendment? As we shall see when we look at the Due Process of Law Clause in the context of prisons, the courts have simply ignored the "involuntary servitude" provision of the Thirteenth Amendment.

In order to apply the Eighth Amendment's cruel and unusual punishment clause to regulate medical care in prisons, the Court reasoned as follows:

> the primary concern of the drafters was to proscribe "tortures" and other "barbarous" methods of punishment [50 L Ed 2d, at p. 258].
>
> Our more recent cases ... have held that the Amendment proscribes more than physically barbarous punishments....
>
> we have held repugnant to the Eighth Amendment punishments which are incompatible with "the evolving standards of decency that mark the progress of a maturing society" ... or which involve the unnecessary and wanton infliction of pain [50 L Ed 2d, at p. 259].

The Court drew these pronouncements from a case upholding a second electrocution after the first had accidentally failed; a case upholding the death penalty in general, and the Georgia procedure for imposing it in particular; a case declaring loss of citizenship upon conviction by court martial and dishonorable discharge for deserting the armed services in time of war to be cruel and unusual punishment; and the *Weems* case (15 years in chains in prison, etc.).

The words "unnecessary and wanton infliction of pain" came from a case in which the question was whether a sentence of death inflicted cruel and unusual punishment.

All of these cases dealt with the terms of sentences imposed by courts and with the statutes on which these sentences were based. None of these cases had anything to do with living conditions in prison in general, or prison medical care in particular.

But relying on the general words it had quoted, the Court went on to say:

> These elementary principles establish the government's obligation to provide medical care for those whom it is punishing by incarceration. An inmate must rely on prison authorities to treat his medical needs ... failure [to do so] may actually produce physical "torture or lingering death"...
>
> The infliction of such unnecessary suffering is inconsistent with contemporary standards of decency....
>
> We therefore conclude that deliberate indifference to serious medical needs of prisoners constitutes the "unnecessary and wanton infliction of pain" ... proscribed by the Eighth Amendment [50 L Ed 2d, at p. 259–260].

But the Eighth Amendment does not contain the words "unnecessary and wanton infliction of pain." It prohibits "cruel and unusual punishments." By substituting the word "unnecessary," the Court gave itself the power to determine what conditions of imprisonment are "necessary," how much medical care is "necessary," and so on.

Undoubtedly, neglecting medical care in prisons would be inhumane, but until *Estelle v. Gamble* the legislative and executive branches determined what was "necessary" or "unnecessary" in the prisons. As a matter of fact, the Texas legislature had considered a hospital, doctors, medical assistants, and nurses necessary, so they were there when Gamble hurt his back, and they gave him treatment and medicines.

The Court outlined what it considered a violation of the constitutional right it had created in the *Estelle* case:

> a complaint that a physician has been negligent in diagnosing or treating a medical condition does not state a valid claim for medical mistreatment under the Eighth Amendment. Medical malpractice does

not become a constitutional violation merely because the victim is a prisoner ... a prisoner must allege acts or omissions sufficiently harmful to evidence deliberate indifference to serious medical needs [50 L Ed 2d, at p. 261].

The Court then looked at the actual facts of Gamble's medical case, and concluded that Gamble did not have a case under the Court's standards for a constitutional violation. Whether the prison doctors should or should not have taken X-rays of Gamble's lower back was a "classic example of a matter for medical judgment," and a decision not to take X-rays was not cruel and unusual punishment.

So Gamble's complaint against the doctors was thrown out. But the new constitutional rule, which the Court had created in this case, remained as a precedent, giving the Court and the lower federal courts the power to determine, in future cases, not merely whether a given sentence of imprisonment was "cruel and unusual," but whether any incident occurring during such imprisonment showed "deliberate indifference" to serious needs of a prisoner. Thus the Court, in effect, amended the Eighth Amendment by adding: "nor imprisonment administered with deliberate indifference to a prisoner's serious needs."

Serious medical needs were the beginning. By 1992 the rule had been expanded to cover the use of force by prison guards. Use of force was considered to be "cruel and unusual punishment" when the Court considered it "unnecessary," even if the prisoner did not suffer "serious injury." The courts, not the prison administrators, would decide what force was necessary (*Hudson v. McMillan* [1992] 503 US 1, 117 L Ed 2d 156, 112 S Ct 995).

Two justices dissented:

> a use of force that causes only insignificant harm to a prisoner may be immoral, it may be tortious, it may be criminal, and it may even be remedial under other provisions of the Federal Constitution, but it is not "cruel and unusual punishment." In concluding to the contrary, the Court today goes far beyond our precedents [117 L Ed 2d, at p. 173].

After reviewing the history of the Eighth Amendment the dissent concluded:

> Today's expansion of the Cruel and Unusual Punishment Clause beyond all bounds of history and precedent is, I suspect, yet another manifestation of the pervasive view that the Federal Constitution

must address all ills in our society. Abusive behavior by prison guards is deplorable conduct that properly provokes outrage and contempt. But that does not mean that it is invariably unconstitutional. The Eighth Amendment is not, and should not be turned into, a National Code of Prison Regulation. To reject the notion that the infliction of concededly "minor" injuries can be considered either "cruel" or "unusual" punishment ... is not to say that it amounts to acceptable conduct. Rather, it is to recognize that primary responsibility for preventing and punishing such conduct rests not with the Federal Constitution but with the laws and regulations of the various States [117 L Ed 2d, at p. 179–180].

But a year later the majority of the Court expanded the Court's power over prisons even further.

In *Helling v. McKinney* (1993) 509 US 25, 125 L Ed 2d 22, 113 S Ct 2475, the Court held that exposing a prisoner "to levels of ETS [environmental tobacco smoke] that pose an unreasonable risk of serious damage to his future health" (125 L Ed 2d, at p. 33) violates the Eighth Amendment, if the risk is so grave that it violates contemporary standards of decency" (125 L Ed 2d, at p. 33).

The Court would, of course, have to decide what these standards are.

Again, two justices dissented:

In *Hudson*, the Court extended *Estelle* to cases in which the prisoner has suffered only minor injuries; here, it extends *Estelle* to cases in which there has been no injury at all.... I would draw the line at actual, serious injuries and reject the claim that exposure to the risk of injury can violate the Eighth Amendment [125 L Ed 2d, at p. 37].

More recently, the expansion of the reach of the Eighth Amendment slowed down a bit. In *Farmer v. Brennan* (1994) 511 US 825, 128 L Ed 2d 811, 114 S Ct 1970, the Court held that there was not "deliberate indifference," if the prison official in question was not actually aware of the risk to the prisoner(128 L Ed 2d, at p. 825). One of the justices who had dissented in *Hudson* and in *Helling* , held on to the view that the Eighth Amendment does not regulate "prison conditions not imposed as part of a sentence" (128 L Ed 2d at p. 840) and urged the Court to overrule *Estelle v. Gamble*, the case in which the Court had, in effect, amended the Eighth Amendment.

There the matter stands today. The Eighth Amendment is still a National Code of Prison Regulation dictated by the federal courts to

State prisons. In that function the Eighth Amendment is supplemented by the Due Process of Law Clause of the Fourteenth Amendment, which provides:

> nor shall any State deprive any person of ... liberty ... without due process of law.

In plain English these words mean that a state may deprive a person of liberty, if it is done with due process of law. The Thirteenth Amendment says:

> Neither slavery nor involuntary servitude, except as a punishment for crime whereof the party shall have been duly convicted, shall exist within the United States.

Simply, these words mean that a criminal who has been "duly convicted" may be punished with "involuntary servitude." "Duly" obviously refers to *due* process of law.

So, if due process has been observed at the trial, and all reviews of the case by higher courts have been concluded, the criminal may be deprived of liberty, placed into involuntary servitude, and there's an end to it, as far as the federal Constitution is concerned, one might think. It would then be up to the people in the various states to decide, in accordance with their consciences and standards of decency, how to treat their criminals while in prison. But the reality is different.

It is said that fish caught and killed by sport fishermen are known to have an afterlife in which they continue to grow. The same may be said about the liberty protected by the Due (process of) Law Clause. It keeps growing after conviction despite the fact that the prisoner has been deprived of it. The criminal, who has seriously broken the social contract, by, perhaps, murdering your father, raping your mother, kidnapping and torturing your sister, robbing and crippling your brother, when found guilty, used to be called a convict. Now he turns into an "inmate," with all the connotations of friendly fellowship the word "mate" carries with it. An "inmate," even though he has seriously breached the social contract, draws constitutional rights from that very social contract that he breached—so the courts tell us—despite the Thirteenth Amendment.

What happened to "involuntary servitude" as punishment for crime?

141

One federal court of appeals had this to say about the matter:

> The Thirteenth Amendment, if read literally, suggests that the States may treat their prisoners as slaves...
>
> However, by emphasizing the applicability to state prisoners of the Fourteenth Amendment, which now incorporates most of the Bill of Rights including the Eighth Amendment's prohibition of "cruel and unusual punishments," courts in recent years have moderated the harsh implications of the Thirteenth Amendment. But the tension remains between the view that a prisoner enjoys many constitutional rights, which rights can be limited only to the extent necessary for the maintenance of a person's status as prisoner ... and the view that a prisoner has only a few rudimentary rights and must accept whatever regulations and restrictions prison administrators and State law deem essential to a correctional system [*Morales v. Schmidt* (1973) 489 F 2d 1335, at p. 1338].

There it is: Courts have "moderated" the "harshness." How have they "moderated" it? They have done it by "emphasizing" that the Fourteenth Amendment applies to state prisoners. But all the Fourteenth says is that they may be deprived of liberty, after due process has been observed. There is not a word in the Fourteenth saying what happens *after* they have been deprived of their liberty. In plain English "deprived" means it is gone. So how does that change what the Thirteenth Amendment says about involuntary servitude as punishment for crime?

Never mind. We say that "due ... law" applies even after conviction and that cancels out involuntary servitude, and since we have the ultimate say about what the Constitution means, we have the power to tell the States what law is due in their prisons. Thus we have moderated the harsh implications of the Thirteenth Amendment.

In the Supreme Court cases which created what may be called the "Inmates' Bill of Rights," I have found one reference to the Punishment for Crime Exception of the Thirteenth Amendment. One justice, dissenting from a decision which he felt did not favor inmates sufficiently, quoted with approval from *Morales v. Schmidt* that "courts in recent years have moderated the harsh implications of the Thirteenth Amendment" (*Meachum v. Fano* [1976] 427 US 215, 49 L Ed 2d 451, at p. 463, 96 S Ct 2532).

That appears to be the only reference to the Punishment for Crime Exception in the Supreme Court's prison conditions—due process of law cases. The Court has, in effect, amended the Thirteenth Amendment by deleting the words "except as punishment for crime whereof the party shall have been duly convicted."

It may well be that a majority of the citizens of the United States would agree with this informal amendment of the Thirteenth Amendment, if they became aware of this fact. But it might also be that they would resent this stroke of a pen by which state prison systems, without visible support in the Constitution, and contrary to the Thirteenth Amendment's express words, became subject to supervision by the federal courts.

The issue is not whether prisoners in State prisons should be ill treated or not. No one argues that they should be ill treated. The issue is whether prisoners in State prisons after being "duly convicted" of crime and placed into "involuntary servitude" retain *federal* constitutional rights.

As we have seen, one federal constitutional right is implied in the Thirteenth Amendment itself: Since involuntary servitude shall *not exist within the United States*, except as punishment for crime whereof the party shall have been *duly convicted*, a person *not* duly convicted must have access to the federal courts to determine that fact.

If you assume, as the Court does (see *Louisiana ex rel. Francis v. Resweber* [1947] 329 US 459, 91 L Ed 422, 67 S Ct 374; *Robinson v. California* [1962] 370 US 660, 8 L Ed 2d 758) that the Eighth Amendment applies to the states, then there must also be access to the federal courts to determine whether the punishment imposed by the sentence of a state court is "cruel and unusual."

Congress has given convicted state prisoners the statutory right to petition the federal courts for the writ of habeas corpus to determine whether a state court has followed due process of law in convicting the prisoner and whether the state court sentence is "cruel and unusual." If the federal court determines that the state prisoner's petition has no merit, because due process of law has been followed and because the sentence imposed is not cruel and unusual, then the state prisoner has been properly deprived of his liberty and may now properly be placed into involuntary servitude.

At this point the text of the federal Constitution does not give him any further constitutional rights—if it were not for the afterlife of the Due ____ Law Clause.

We have seen (Chapter II) that the Court has created what amounts to a Bill of Individual Liberties of free citizens. The Court created the power to do so by dropping the words "process of" from the Due Process of Law Clause of the Fourteenth Amendment, resulting in what you may call the Due ＿＿ Law Clause.

It is well settled that the Court has the last word on what the Constitution means, and if the Fourteenth Amendment says (as amended by the Court) "nor shall any state deprive any person of ... liberty ... without due ＿＿ law," and if the Punishment Exception of the Thirteenth Amendment is ignored, then the Court can say "liberty" means some but not all liberty and it isn't due law if a State takes away all liberty, and the Court will tell the States how much liberty is still due after conviction.

By these means the Court created an "Inmates' Bill of Rights" giving convicted criminals some procedural and some substantive constitutional rights.

This was done in a sequence of cases beginning in the 1970s. The convicts' rights range from substantial religious freedom, freedom of speech, the right to petition the government for grievances (*Wolff v. McDonnell* [1974] 418 US 539, 41 L Ed 2d 935, at p. 950–951, 94 S Ct 2963) to the right of access to the federal courts to claim "liberty interests" such as a "liberty interest in a waiver of the travel limit imposed on prison furloughs," a "liberty interest in receiving a tray lunch rather than a sack lunch," a "liberty interest in receiving a paperback dictionary due to a rule that states a prisoner 'may receive any book ... which does not present a threat to the order or security of the institution,'" a "liberty interest in freedom from transfer to a smaller cell without electrical outlets for televisions and liberty interest in a prison job," a "liberty interest in not being placed on a foodloaf diet" (*Sandin v. Conner* [1995] 515 US 472, 132 L Ed 2d 418, at p. 429, 115 S Ct 2293).

The author has not bothered to check how many of these claims were granted and how many were thrown out. As I see it, the problem is that such cases get into federal court in the first place, and, to add insult to injury, the courts may award attorneys' fees against the state (which is to say the taxpayer), if the prisoner wins (*Martin v. Hadix* [1999] 527 US 343, 144 L Ed 2d 347, at p. 354, 119 S Ct 1998), as did the "no food loaf diet" claimant.

The right of access to the courts includes the right to a law library, which the State must supply, "or adequate assistance from persons trained in the law," and also access to fellow prisoners known as "jailhouse lawyers" or "writ writers" (*Bounds v. Smith* [1977] 430 US 817, 52 L Ed 2d 72, at p. 83, 97 S Ct 1491).

To get a feel for what these court-created constitutional rights mean, the dissenting opinions of some Supreme Court justices are of great help. In *Bounds v. Smith*, three justices in three dissenting opinions strongly questioned the Court's creation of a federal constitutional right to state prison law libraries.

One justice said

> There is nothing in the United States Constitution which requires that a convict serving a term of imprisonment pursuant to a final judgment of a court of competent jurisdiction in a state penal institution have a "right of access" to the federal courts in order to attack his sentence [*Bounds v. Smith*, 52 L Ed 2d, at p. 89].

Another justice said

> absent a federal constitutional right to attack convictions collaterally—and I discern no such right—I can find no basis on which a federal court may require States to fund costly law libraries for prison inmates.
> ...whatever right exists is solely a creation of a federal statute [*Bounds v. Smith*, 52 L Ed 2d, at p. 87].

Both justices said that there is nothing in the federal Constitution to give state prisoners a federal constitutional right of access to the federal courts to challenge their state convictions.

Both justices recognized that Congress has, by the Habeas Corpus statute (28 USCA Section 2241 and following) given state prisoners a *statutory* right to challenge their state convictions.

If the access right is not given by the Constitution, but only by federal statute, the dissenting justices reasoned, then you cannot say that the Constitution requires the States to provide prison law libraries. Congress would have no power to impose such an obligation on the states, only the Constitution could.

Note that the two justices did not find a constitutional right of federal court access for determining whether prisoners are "duly" held in "involuntary servitude," which seems to be implied in the Punishment Exception of the Thirteenth Amendment. But that may simply be due to the fact that the Punishment Exception is sort of a Lord Voldemort (see *Harry Potter* book series, or ask your preteens or your grandkids) in the judicial world: IT, you know which, whose name must never be mentioned.

As to the "writ writers," another dissent describes some of the abuses:

> [this] type of writ-writer ... writes writs for economic gain. This group is composed of a few unscrupulous manipulators who are interested only in acquiring from other prisoners money, cigarettes or merchandise purchased in the inmate canteen. Once they have a client's interest aroused and determine his ability to pay, they must keep him on the "hook." This is commonly done by deliberately misstating the facts of his case so that it appears, at least on the surface, that the inmate is entitled to relief. The documents drafted for the client cast the writ-writer in the role of a sympathetic protagonist. After reading them, the inmate is elated that he has found someone able to present his case favorably. He is willing to pay to maintain the lie that has been created for him.

And this is how the resources of our federal courts are wasted by the frivolous:

> When decisions do not help a writ-writer, he may employ a handful of tricks.... One writ-writer simply made up his own legal citations when he ran short of actual ones. In one action against the California Adult Authority involving the application of administrative law, one writ-writer used the following citations: *Aesop v. Fables, First Baptist Church v. Sally Stanford, Doda v. One Firty-Four* [sic] *Inch Chest,* and *Dogood v. The Planet Earth.* The references to the volume and page numbers of the nonexistent publications were equally fantastic, such as 901 Penal Review, page 17,240. To accompany each case, he composed an eloquent decision which, if good law, would make selected acts of the Adult Authority unconstitutional. In time the "decisions" freely circulated among other writ-writers, and several gullible ones began citing them also [*Cruz v. Beto* (1972) 405 US 319, 31 L Ed 2d 263, at p. 271, footnote 7, quoting from a law review article, 92 S Ct 1079].

The Supreme Court's intentions in creating the "Inmates' Bill of Rights" under the Due ____ Law Clause were, no doubt, the best, but something may be amiss here, beyond the abuses.

A majority of the citizens of this country may wonder whether prisoners are really "due" such federal "constitutional" rights.

Take prisoner medical care, for which, as we have seen, a state may be held liable as a matter of federal constitutional law (*Estelle v. Gamble* [1976] 50 L Ed 2d 251). The reasoning by which the Court found this right to be due to prisoners as a federal constitutional right was, ironically, drawn from a state court decision. The quote is: "[i]t is but just that the public be required to care for the prisoners, who cannot, by reason of the deprivation of his liberty, care for himself" (50 L Ed 2d, at p. 260).

But is not, for example, a victim crippled by the prisoner's crime equally unable to care for himself, especially if the victim is poor? If the prisoner has a federal constitutional right to medical care, why would the victim not have at least the same right? Yet under "well-settled" law the state is not liable for failing to protect the victim from the criminal.

It is, undoubtedly, humane if the public provides prison medical care, but is it "but just" to provide such care to the criminal and not to the victim?

One more example: Freedom of Speech. The First Amendment says: "Congress shall make no law ... abridging the freedom of speech." How do you find in these words a federal constitutional right of freedom of speech for duly convicted state prisoners serving their term of involuntary servitude?

During the years of communist agitation after the First World War, when many states enacted statutes prohibiting various forms of communist activity, the United States Supreme Court decided that the "liberty" protected against state action by the Due (process of) Law Clause included the freedom of speech protected by the First Amendment against Congress. At issue were the rights of free citizens to advocate "social, economic and political doctrine which a vast majority of ... citizens believes to be false and fraught with evil consequences" (*Whitney v. California* [1927] 274 US 357, at p. 374).

Justice Brandeis, joined by Justice Holmes, stated the reasons which eventually (see, for example, *Stromberg v. California* [1931] 283 US 359, at p. 368) led the Court to hold that freedom of speech is part of the liberty protected by Due (process of) Law:

> all fundamental rights comprised within the term liberty are protected by the Federal Constitution from invasion by the States. The right of free speech, the right to teach and the right of assembly are, of course, fundamental rights [274 US, at p. 373].
>
> Those who won our independence believed ... that freedom to think as you will and to speak as you think are means indispensable to the discovery of political truth ... that public discussion is a political duty ... that the path of safety lies in the opportunity to discuss freely supposed grievances and proposed remedies.... Believing in the

power of reason as applied through public discussion, they eschewed silence coerced by law—the argument of force in its worst form [274 US, at p. 375–376].

Because freedom of speech is an essential right of free citizens and an essential part of self-government by free citizens the Court found it to be part of the liberty which is protected against state action which abridges political speech.

But when a person has seriously breached the social contract, has been duly convicted, and has been deprived of liberty for the duration of his term of involuntary servitude, why should he be given back the freedom of speech? To participate with free citizens in the self-government of a free community from which he has excluded himself by deliberate action?

A majority of citizens may feel that these are matters which should have been left to the people of the various states acting through their representatives, which is where the U.S. Constitution had left them during the first 180 years of the Republic.

To be sure, the prison conditions which first led the federal courts to intervene, beginning in 1970, were atrocious, barbarous, inhumane. (See for example, *Hutton v. Finney* [1976] 429 US 97, 50 L Ed 2d 251, at p. 528–530 [including footnotes 3, 4, 5, 6, 7), 97 S Ct 285 (Arkansas penal system), and *Rhodes v. Chapman* (1981) 452 US 337, 69 L Ed 2d 59, at p. 74-75 [including footnote 3], 101 S Ct 2392 [Alabama penal system].)

No civilized citizen who reads the descriptions of prison life given in these cases would wish to return prisons to the conditions then prevailing.

Yet, by in effect amending the Eighth, Thirteenth and Fourteenth Amendments a door to abuses in the other direction was opened. It is possible to be too humane.

- The new Eighth Amendment:
   "nor cruel and unusual punishment inflicted," <u>nor imprisonment administered with deliberate indifference to a prisoner's serious needs</u>."
- The new Thirteenth Amendment:
   "neither slavery nor involuntary servitude, _____, shall exist within the United States"
- The new Fourteenth Amendment:
   "nor shall any state deprive any person of ... liberty ... without due ____ law; <u>provided, however, that "liberty" shall mean some but not all liberty</u>."

Congress has reined in some of the abuses by the Prison Litigation Reform Act of 1995 (110 Stat. 1321–1366, 42 USCA Section 1997[e]), and the Court, as we have seen, has slowed down the expansion of the reach of the Eighth Amendment in *Farmer v. Brennan* (1994) 511 US 825, 128 L Ed 2d 811, 114 S Ct 1970. But a majority of citizens might well wish to have some means by which they can control interpretations of the Constitution which tend to treat prisoners more and more like free citizens, merely subject to the temporary inconvenience of incarceration.

One justice, in a dissenting opinion, said:

> the punishment which a criminal conviction entails do[es] not place the citizen beyond the ethical tradition that accords respect to the dignity and intrinsic worth of every individual. "Liberty" and "custody" are not mutually exclusive concepts [*Meachum v. Fano* (1976) 427 US 215, 49 L Ed 2d 451, at p. 463–464, 96 S Ct 2532].

> each individual retains his dignity and, in time, acquires a status that is entitled to respect [49 L Ed 2d at p. 465].

Conceivably, a majority of citizens might not see such "intrinsic worth" or "dignity" in a dangerous criminal, or wish to accord such "respect," to a murderer, robber or rapist, or even a confirmed swindler, especially as long as nothing is "found" in the Constitution protecting the intrinsic worth and dignity of the victims of crime.

To a lawyer this may sound ludicrous, but to a common sense citizen, if the Constitution "says" that a convicted criminal has a constitutional right to medical care, yet his victim has no such constitutional right, that does not sound like "equal protection of the laws."

Chapter XI

What Can and
Should We Do?

We have seen that Congress and the Court have effectively amended the Constitution in various ways. Congress has created "big government." Do we want to do something about this? If so, what?

In recent years several constitutional amendments addressing the problem of "big government" have been proposed or discussed. There is, of course, the balanced budget amendment. In addition, a term limits amendment, a line item veto amendment, a school prayer amendment, a prohibition of unfunded mandates amendment, an amendment allowing three fourths of the states to repeal federal laws that unduly burden them, an amendment to create a California style initiative power on the national level, and an as yet undefined amendment to check the growth of government by tax limitations have been discussed (*The Wall Street Journal*, 23 November 1994, "Rule of Law," by Terry Eastland; 25 November 1994, "Potomac Watch," by Paul A. Gigot; 1 June 1998, "Will Politicians Take the Initiative," by John H. Fund; 5 June 1998, "Whither the Tax Revolt," by Amity Shlaes.)

This book proposes a constitutional amendment which will provide a procedure for exercising the citizens' power to correct an *interpretation* of the Constitution with which they do not agree. By a vote of the majority in each of a majority of the states, they could enact a "Declaration of True Meaning."

Unlike most of the proposals mentioned above, this corrective declaration by ballot is aimed at involving the citizens directly, as does an initiative procedure. The citizens' corrective declaration would be a power to repeal, overrule, or modify any official act of the federal

150

government which the voters believed rested on an erroneous interpretation of the Constitution.

The declaration would *not amend* the Constitution. It is not intended to substitute direct democracy for our system of representative democracy. But the functioning of our system could be improved through occasional direct, but limited, action by the citizens.

What form should the citizens' power to pass corrective declarations take? As we have seen in Chapter II, the genius of our court-made law is to progress in small steps based on experience rather than mere logic. The citizens' corrective declaration by ballot could work in a similar way. It would not be in lieu of the existing amendment provisions of the Constitution, which remain as the sole means of formally changing the text of the Constitution; it would be in addition to these provisions. A citizens' corrective declaration would only repeal, restrict or expand, in whole or in part, an interpretation of the text of the Constitution by Congress, the president, the courts, or the agencies. It is not intended to change the text of the Constitution.

The Framers saw the remedy for unconstitutional acts of the government in the election of "more faithful representatives" (*The Federalist*, No. 44). But we have since found that it is impractical to elect representatives on a single issue. We cannot hope to resolve constitutional questions through the election of representatives. This was recognized early on:

> it is obvious, that elections can rarely, if ever, furnish any sufficient proofs, what is deliberately the will of the people, as to any constitutional or legal doctrines. Representatives and rulers must be ordinarily chosen for very different purposes; and, in many instances, their opinions upon constitutional questions must be unknown to their constituents. The only means known to the Constitution, by which to ascertain the will of the people upon a constitutional question, is in the shape of an affirmative or negative proposition by way of amendment [Kurland, Vol. 4, p. 206, No. 38, Story, *Commentaries on the Constitution* (1833)].

The citizens' corrective declaration would provide the means to correct instances of government overreaching which do not warrant an amendment of the Constitution.

To give us this power an amendment would have to be added to the Constitution. This might become the Twenty-eighth Amendment.

How do we go about it? We will have to write to our senators and representatives and ask them to propose an amendment to the Constitution. If two thirds of all representatives and two thirds of all senators "deem it necessary" the amendment will be proposed. Then it will take the legislatures of three fourths of the states to make the amendment effective. That can take awhile.

Don't despair. Until 1913, U.S. senators were chosen by the state legislatures. But in the years preceding 1913, enough citizens raised their voices about this that the Seventeenth Amendment, providing for election of U.S. senators directly by the citizens, was adopted by Congress in 1912, with the strong support of President William H. Taft. It became effective a year later. (*The Oxford History of the American People*, by Samuel Eliot Morison, New York, Oxford University Press, 1965, reprinted with corrections, 1972, at p. 833.)

Election of senators directly by the citizens, and correction of errors in the interpretation of the Constitution directly by the citizens, are examples of citizens retaining ultimate control over their government. This is our birthright, or, for the naturalized citizen, our right by way of adoption.

The amendment giving us the procedure to correct misinterpretations of the Constitution might be phrased like this:

AMENDMENT XXVIII

1. The citizens of the United States may repeal, overrule, or modify any official act or acts of the Congress, the president, the courts, or any other branch, agency, or entity of the federal government, by declaring what the relevant words of this Constitution mean, or do not mean.

2. When, in each state, fifty thousand citizens, entitled to vote, have signed a Declaration of True Meaning, the declaration shall be placed on the ballot for the next election of members of the House of Representatives.

3. When a majority of the citizens voting in such election have voted in favor of the declaration in each state of four fifths of the several states, the declaration, until deleted or changed by another declaration, shall be the definitive interpretation of this Constitution, and shall become effective at midnight on the day of the election, but not retroactive from that day.

4. A Declaration of True Meaning shall overrule or modify a final court decision as precedent only.

5. Congress shall, within twelve months from the day of the election, refund to the citizens who are natural persons and taxpayers, in equal shares, all monies appropriated during that fiscal year in connection with any official act which has been repealed by a Declaration of True Meaning.

6. A Declaration of True Meaning shall not be reviewed as to its validity by any court, federal or state, except to determine whether the required number of citizens have signed and voted.

Two and a half million citizens nationwide agreeing that a matter should be put to a vote assures that a Declaration of True Meaning will be of true concern. This would not be a mere poll. The number of votes cast in the election, even if not sufficient to carry the measure, would show the sense of the nation on the particular issue, to Congress, to the president, to the Court or any other branch, agency or entity of the government.

It is likely that a Declaration of True Meaning on a given issue signed by two and a half million citizens would send a message to Congress about that issue, long before it is even put to the vote.

The number of fifty thousand citizens per state was chosen to make it relatively easy to start the corrective process. There may be hundreds of proposed declarations in a given year. The more the merrier. We must re-argue and re-decide the old questions of the scope of the Constitution, of the limits of congressional, presidential, or judicial power, or we will lose control of our government.

It has been observed that our government has become "a sprawling, largely self-organizing structure that is 10% to 20% under the control of the politicians and voters and 80% to 90% under the countless thousands of client groups" (*The Wall Street Journal*, 14 April 1998, "Demosclerosis Returns," by Jonathan Rauch).

To the same effect:

> The unlimiting of government has invited more and more interest groups to feed at its trough, and legislators have made increasingly longer careers out of distributing the feed.... We the people are the "special interests" ... we too are part ... of bigger, more intrusive, more expensive government" [*The Wall Street Journal*, 23 November 1994, "To Amend, or Not to Amend," by Terry Eastland].

Pogo's immortal words sum up the situation: "We have met the enemy, and they are us." Do we have to resign ourselves to this? Some people think there is no way out:

The public and political activists are growing gradually, if grudgingly, more accepting of the natural limits on government's ability to change society. Now they need to begin accepting the limits on society's ability to change the government [*The Wall Street Journal*, "Demosclerosis Returns"].

It remains to be seen, if some of the laws of doubtful constitutional validity which sustain the "client groups" and the "special interests" of big government cannot be brought into the public view, one by one, and, after a vigorous public debate, be voted up or down on a Declaration of True Meaning.

Under the existing amendment provisions of the Constitution, "[s]ince 1791, more than 10,700 amendments have been introduced in Congress, but only 33 have been proposed to the states and just 27 have been ratified" (*The Wall Street Journal*, "To Amend, or Not to Amend").

No perceptible harm has come to the republic from the debate on the 10,673 or more proposals which did not make it. However, they took up congressional working time. Debates on Declarations of True Meaning would be outside of Congress, outside of the government. Instead of weasel-worded polls, clear issues and more than a statistical sample of citizens would necessarily be involved.

The requirement of a majority of the voters *in each State* of four fifths of the States is to protect the people in the less populous states from being overwhelmed by the voters of a few populous states. The Constitution was intended to protect the interests of all citizens and regions of the country and not merely the interests of a few populous states or regions. Every state, however small its population, was given two senators by the Founders for that reason.

Nothing is perfect. Prohibition was brought in by a formal constitutional amendment. Similar mistakes might be made with a citizens' Declaration of True Meaning. But a mistaken Declaration could probably be corrected more quickly than was Prohibition.

The effective date of a Declaration of True Meaning, election day, provides a clear cut-off. The Constitution contains express provisions against certain types of retroactive laws (Article II, Section 9, Clause 3, and Section 10, Clause 1). Paragraph 3 of the proposal would avoid conflict with these provisions by prohibiting retroactivity in any form.

Paragraph 3 also makes clear that a Declaration of True Meaning is not an amendment to the text of the Constitution, and therefore may be removed by another declaration without following the amendment procedures of Article V of the Constitution.

Paragraph 4 of the proposal expressly recognizes the well-established judicial tradition, that a final judgment of a court, once all methods of review have been exhausted, remains final and binding on the parties to the suit.

Paragraph 5 of the proposal would put teeth into the citizens' interpretations of the Constitution. Once a law has been repealed as unconstitutional by a Declaration of True Meaning, that law would be void. An expenditure of money under a void law would be illegal and an impeachable offense. But you cannot impeach a majority of Congress. So a watershed event is needed to show the voters whether a majority of Congress is flouting the Constitution. A failure to refund, within 12 months from the day of the election, the money appropriated for the void program for the fiscal year in which the election was held would be such a watershed event.

By election day, the budget for the then current fiscal year would normally have been enacted. We assume that Congress will raise only the revenue needed for the lawful purposes specified in the budget. When the citizens declare that one of those purposes is unconstitutional, it follows that the revenue to pay for it was or would be raised illegally and must be returned to the citizens.

To curtail, somewhat, the influence corporations might try to exercise in connection with a Declaration of True Meaning, no refund to corporations is provided. The matter is between the individual citizens and their government.

Distribution in equal shares to individual citizen taxpayers should be easy to administer: divide the appropriation in question by the number of citizen taxpayers on individual income tax returns, type the check for the amount (it would be the same amount for everyone) and put it into the mail. Since the matter is one between the citizens and their government, it's no business of any aliens.

Paragraph 6 of the proposal makes clear that the citizens have the last word on the Constitution. We have seen how Thomas Jefferson, Andrew Jackson, and Abraham Lincoln expressed doubts about the propriety of a few unelected persons, namely the Court, having the final say about the meaning of the Constitution. Similar doubts were expressed even before the Constitution had been adopted. In 1788, the publicist writing under the name of "Brutus" warned about the power to be given to the judiciary by the proposed Constitution:

> It is, moreover, of great importance, to examine with care the nature and extent of the judicial power, because those who are to be vested with it, are to be placed in a situation altogether unprecedented in a free country. They are to be rendered totally independent, both of the people and the legislature.... No errors they may commit can be corrected by any power above them, if any such power there be, nor can they be removed from office for making ever so many erroneous adjudications....
>
> The opinions of the supreme court, whatever they may be, will have the force of law; because there is no power provided in the constitution, that can correct their errors, or controul [sic] their adjudications. From this court there is no appeal [Kurland, Vol. 4, pp. 235, 236, No. 19].

Echoing this age old concern, in 1912 President Theodore Roosevelt proposed that the people should have the power of the referendum "in a certain class of decisions of constitutional questions." Roosevelt said:

> My proposal is that the people shall have the power to decide for themselves, in the last resort, what legislation is necessary in exercising the police powers, the general welfare powers, so as to give expression to the general morality, the general opinion, of the people. In England ... no one dreams that the court has a right to express an opinion in such matters as against the will of the people shown by the action of the legislature. I do not propose to go as far as this, I do not propose to do in these matters what England, Canada, Australia, and France have always done, that is, make the legislature supreme over the courts in these cases, I merely propose to make legislature and court alike responsible to the sober and deliberate judgment of the people, who are masters of both legislature and courts. This proposal is precisely and exactly in line with Lincoln's attitude toward the Supreme Court in the Dred Scott case, and with the doctrines he laid down for the rule of the people in his first inaugural as President.
> [*The Writings of Theodore Roosevelt*, edited by William H. Harbaugh, Indianapolis: Bobbs-Merrill, 1967, at p. 271].

The Declaration of True Meaning procedure would give us, the majority of the citizens, a practical means to directly exercise the power of last resort which we undoubtedly have under our theory of government. At present, we can exercise it only by persuading two thirds of our representatives in Congress, or two thirds of our state legislatures, to start an amendment, and by prevailing on three fourths of our state legislatures to finally adopt the amendment (Article V of the Constitution). Under the Framers' plan we have no direct vote on an amendment.

The Framers wanted to be sure that an overwhelming majority of the people would desire an amendment before it moved forward. That was and is sound; the Constitution should not lightly be amended.

But the Framers did not foresee the process by which Congress and the Court have, in effect, amended and are amending the Constitution by small increments. The Declaration of True Meaning procedure would give us a means to counter and control these numerous, small, creeping, "informal amendments" if we find them unacceptable.

As to the words which people will use to draft such declarations, it will go as it has gone with initiatives in California. Long-winded, complicated, obscure documents in legalese have typically been rejected by the voters. Mercifully, Declarations of True Meaning can be short, as some examples will show.

If we succeed in having an amendment adopted which gives us the procedure of the Declaration of True Meaning, how should we use it? There is no need for us to codify those of the congressional and judicial informal amendments to the Constitution discussed earlier, which we accept. So long as everyone understands them for what they are, no change in the constitutional words is needed, as with "army" and "navy."

The useful and practical thing to do is to amend, repeal, or overrule, by Declarations of True Meaning, those informal amendments by Congress or the Court, which we consider to be erroneous interpretations of the Constitution. For example, by changing the phrase "*navigable* waters of the United States," which was the traditional interpretation of the Commerce Clause, to "waters of the United States," Congress created its new power to legislate about all private lands in the United States which are somewhere near a stream, lake or pond, or, if not that, are "wet" all year or some part of a year. The necessary majority of the citizens might want to define "waters of the United States" more carefully, to prevent government control of waters on private lands created for private use, perhaps excluding parcels not exceeding a certain size.

As to the informal amendments we do not accept, repeal or overruling by a Declaration of True Meaning would be in order. For example, the necessary majority of the citizens might think that the Court's (and Congress') newly created power to legislate about abortion should be overruled (and repealed as far as Congress is concerned). This power belonged to the states for the first 184 years of the Republic. Then, in 1973, in *Roe v. Wade* the Supreme Court seized this power. What distinguishes abortion from the individual rights in the Court's great Bill of Individual Liberties is that after 25 years the so-called right to abortion has still not been accepted into our traditions by millions of American citizens. With the benefit of hindsight, it may be said, that this "right" does not even meet the Court's own criteria for creating a new individual right under the Due (process of) Law Clause.

Here is a recent statement, by the Supreme Court, of these criteria:

> We begin, as we do in all due process cases, by examining our Nation's history, legal traditions and practices.... The primary and most reliable indication of [a national] consensus is ... the pattern of enacted laws ... and further ... the Due Process Clause specially protects those fundamental rights and liberties which are, objectively, deeply rooted in this Nation's history and traditions [*Washington v. Glucksberg* (1997) 521 US 702, 138 L Ed 2d 772, at p. 781, p. 787, 117 S Ct 2258].

Was there a body of state legislation favoring abortion when *Roe v. Wade* was decided in 1973? Was a right to abortion then deeply rooted in the American tradition? Does state legislation, even today, show an "acceptance" of this right? The answer is "No."

While yielding to the Supreme Court's abortion decisions, many of the states are trying to limit abortion on demand as much as they are permitted. (See *Voinovich v. Women's Professional Medical Corporation* [1998] 523 US 1036, 140 L Ed 2d 2496, 118 S Ct 1347). *Stenberg v. Carhart* (2000) 530 US 914, 147 L Ed 2d 743, 120 S Ct 2597.)

The lack of acceptance is shown drastically by the fact that some of our citizens have been willing to kill others of our citizens over the issue. Abortion divides us (at any rate large numbers of us) almost as bitterly as did slavery. We have had our John Browns of abortion, though not at Harpers Ferry yet. That is a serious warning.

By contrast, there appear to have been no killings over other individual rights upheld by the Court in its great Bill of Individual Liberties, such as the right to be free from state interference in the marital bedroom, the right to marry, the right to have children, the right to direct the education and upbringing of one's children, and so forth. (See *Washington v. Glucksberg*, 138 L Ed 2d, at p. 787).

The necessary majority of the citizens might think that it would be best for the general welfare and internal peace of the United States to remove power over abortion from the control of the federal government and restore it to the states, so that the people in each state could enact, through their representatives, abortion laws according to their desire and conscience.

A Declaration of True Meaning to give this power back to the states could read thus:

> The words—"nor be deprived of life, liberty, or property, without due process of law" (Fifth Amendment)
>
> —"nor shall any State deprive any person of life, liberty, or property, without due process of law; nor deny to any person within its jurisdiction the equal protection of the laws" (Fourteenth Amendment)
>
> —"The powers not delegated to the United States by the Constitution, nor prohibited by it to the States, are reserved to the States respectively, or to the people" (Tenth Amendment)
> read separately, or read together, do not give the Congress, the President, the courts, or any other branch, agency, or entity of the federal government the power to make any rules related to abortion.
>
> All decisions by federal courts relating to abortion are overruled, including but not limited to *Roe v. Wade* (1973).... [Insert here a list of the most important decisions.]

The Declaration of True Meaning procedure is content neutral. If the necessary majority of the citizens so desired, a Declaration of True Meaning regarding abortion could be the exact opposite of the example given above:

> The words—"nor be deprived of ... liberty ... without due process of law" (Fifth Amendment)
>
> —"nor shall any State deprive any person of ... liberty ... without due process of law; nor deny to any person within its jurisdiction the equal protection of the laws" (Fourteenth Amendment)
> read separately, or read together, give any woman the right to have her fetus killed, at public expense, at any time before it is born alive.

No institution of government, as long as we remain a free country, will be able to dictate morality (or the lack thereof) to the majority of the citizens. The majority of the citizens in each state must take ultimate responsibility for the laws, and that means the minimum rules of morality, under which we live.

To view another example of a possible Declaration of True Meaning, we have seen (Chapter III) that federal power over education, whether exercised under the Equal Protection Clause, or exercised under the Spending Clause, and financed by taxes drawn from the people of the states, may be said *not* to be for the general welfare, because it damages our federal system by interfering with traditional State powers. It diminishes the amount of money available for education by the amount spent for the federal Department of Education and by the amount spent for the additional state administrative costs caused by the federal programs, and it has not improved education overall despite decades of massive spending.

If the necessary majority of the citizens should want to restore to the states their traditional power over education, a Declaration of True Meaning could read thus:

> The words—"The Congress shall have Power to lay and collect Taxes, Duties, Imposts, and Excises, to pay the debts and provide for the common Defence and general Welfare of the United States" (Article I, Section 8, Clause 1)
>
> —"The Congress shall have power to lay and collect taxes on incomes, from whatever source derived" (Sixteenth Amendment)
>
> —"nor shall any State deprive any person of life, liberty, or property, without due process of law; nor deny to any person within its jurisdiction the equal protection of the laws" (Fourteenth Amendment)
>
> read separately, or read together, do not give the Congress, the president, the courts, or any other branch, agency or entity of the federal government the power to appropriate money for education, to be paid to any state or states, or any political subdivision thereof, or to make rules related to education in the several states.
>
> All acts of Congress appropriating money for education, to be paid to any state or states, or any political subdivision thereof, or making any rules related to education in the several states, are repealed, including, but not limited to the Department of Education Organization Act, the Individuals with Disabilities Education Act, the Higher Education Act [Insert here a list of the federal laws appropriating money for payment to the states for education].

This Declaration would leave the federal government free to provide scholarships for individuals, or to expand the service academies, if Congress determined that specialized, technical education for national defense could best be supplied in that way.

In these drafts of Declarations of True Meaning, the word "power" is used because it occurs in Article I, Section 8, Clause 18 (known as the "necessary and proper clause"), with a meaning that includes legislative, judicial and executive powers, and is thus a well understood constitutional term.

We have seen in this book only a few examples of how Congress, or the Court, has gone beyond the common sense meaning of our mutual contract, the Constitution. If you believe that the examples correctly describe what has happened concerning Congress, then you, as a citizen, should take action to restore the balance between the federal and the state governments, which at present is tilted in favor of "big government." If you believe that the examples correctly describe what has happened concerning the Court, then you, as a citizen, should take action to rein in the Court.

We need the power of direct involvement of citizens which the Declaration of True Meaning procedure would give us. Let us see then, whether you agree.

Index

abortion 15, 16, 17, 158, 159
Agricultural Adjustment Act of 1933
36, 40
Amendments to the U.S. Constitution:
Amendment I (Free Speech) 127, 128,
147; Amendment V (Public Use) 50,
55, 81–82, 83, 159; Amendment VIII
(Cruel and Unusual Punishment) 130,
131, 132, 134, 135, 136, 137, 138, 139,
140, 141, 142, 143, 148, 149; Amendment IX (Rights Retained) 15;
Amendment X (Powers Reserved) 37,
43, 159; Amendment XII 26; Amendment XIII (Involuntaray Servitude)
26, 129, 137, 141, 142, 143, 144, 145, 148;
Amendment XIV (Section 1—Due
Process) 14, 16, 17–18, 26, 50, 55, 56,
57–58, 91, 130, 135, 137, 141, 142, 144,
147, 148, 158, 159, 160; Amendment
XIV (Section 1—Equal Protection) 50,
51, 52, 56, 58, 65–66, 68, 70–73, 85,
88, 89, 90, 91, 92, 130, 141, 144, 146,
147, 158; Amendment XIV (Section 2)
52, 53, 54; Amendment XIV (Section
5—Enforcement) 51, 52, 67, 84, 85, 88,
89, 90, 92; Amendment XV (Right to
Vote) 26, 53, 54; Amendment XVI 26,
160; Amendment XVII (Election of
Senators) 53, 152; Amendment XVIII
(Prohibition) 39; Amendment XIX
(Sexual Discrimination in Voting) 26,
53, 54, 68; Amendment XX 26;
Amendment XXIII 26; Amendment
XXIV 26, 54; Amendment XXV 26;
Amendment XXVII 26
Americans with Disabilities Act of 1990
84, 90
arts: fine 122; useful 122

*Babbitt v. Sweet Home Chapter of Com-
munities for a Great Oregon* 111, 113, 114

Bank of the United States 32, 33
Berman v. Parker 83
"Bill of Individual Liberties" 15, 55,
57–58, 143, 158
Bill of Rights 15, 135
Bounds v. Smith 145
Brandeis, Louis D. (Justice of the U.S.
Supreme Court) 147
Brown, John 17
Brown v. Board of Education of Topeka
50, 51
*Brown v. North Carolina Division of
Motor Vehicles* 90

Calder v. Bull 56
Cargill, Inc. v. United States 108
Carter v. Carter Coal Company 35, 36,
119
City of Boerne v. Flores 13, 90, 91, 92
City of Milwaukee v. Illinois 102
class actions 52
Clean Air Act 96, 97, 102, 103, 104
Clean Water Act of 1948 12, 94, 101,
102, 103, 104
Cohens v. Virginia 46
Commerce Clause—U.S. Constitution
12, 31, 35, 36, 38, 39, 40, 42, 43, 84,
85, 86, 87, 88, 95, 96, 101, 102, 107,
108, 110, 111, 114, 115, 117, 118, 119, 120
Constitution, Article I 21; **Section 2** 54,
Clause 3 22, *Clause 5* 22; **Section 3,**
Clause 6 22; **Section 4** 22; **Section 5,**
Clause 1 112; **Section 8,** *Clauses 1–18*
23, 28, 29, 36, 80, *Clause 1* 27, 65, 73,
74, 123, 160, *Clause 2* 77, *Clause 3* 27,
85, 86, *Clause 5* 77, *Clause 8* 122,
Clause 18 26, 27, 32, 160; **Section 9** 16,
Clauses 1,2,8 24; **Section 10,** *Clauses 2,
3* 24
Constitution, Article II 21; **Section 1**
24; **Section 2,** *Clause 2* 24, 112

Constitution, Article III 21, 46; **Section 2**, *Clause 1* 45, *Clause 3* 25, 46; **Section 3** 25

Constitution, Article IV 21, 49; **Section 1** 25; **Section 3**, *Clause 1* 25, *Clause 2* 16, 17, 25, 60, 62, 110

Constitution, Article V 18, 21, 50, 112, 157

Constitution, Article VI 21, 46, *Clause 2* 92

Constitution, Article VII 21, 46

County of Sacramento v. Lewis 57

"court packing plan" 37

Cruel and Unusual Punishment (Amendment 8) 130, 131, 134, 135, 136, 137, 138, 139, 140, 142, 149

Cruz v. Beto 146

Delhi Sands Flower-Loving Fly 114, 115, 118, 119

Department of Education Organization Act 69

Department of Housing and Urban Development 77

District of Columbia Redevelopment Act of 1945 82

Dred Scott v. Sanford 16, 17, 50, 56, 57

Dressman v. Costle 96

Endangered Species Act of 1966 110

Endangered Species Act of 1969 110

Endangered Species Act of 1973 110, 111, 112, 120

English Bill of Rights 132

enumerated powers—U.S. Constitution 9, 22–26

Environmental Protection Agency (EPA) 94, 96, 97, 98, 99, 100, 104

EPA v. Brown 98

Equal Educational Opportunities Act of 1974 65, 67

Estelle v. Gamble 136, 138, 140, 146

extra-constitutional government 100

Fair Labor Standards Act of 1938 40

Farmer v. Brennan 149

Federal Board for Vocational Education 63

federal-state co-operation 64, 72

The Federalist (Hamilton, Jay, Madison) 10

"Federalists" 29, 30, 31

Fowler v. Lindsay 46

Garrett v. Board of Trustees of the University of Alabama 90

General Welfare Clause *see* Taxing for the General Welfare Clause

general welfare (sum of goodness) 75, 79, 80, 81, 83, 125, 128

Gettysburg Address 53

Gibbons v. Ogden 102

Grant, Ulysses S. 74

Great Depression 34, 39

Gun-Free School Zones Act of 1991 41

Habeas Corpus statute 145

Hamilton, Alexander (first U.S. Secretary of the Treasury) 29, 32, 33, 36, 37, 44

Harlan, John Marshall (1833–1911) (U.S. Supreme Court Justice) 51

Harlan, John Marshall (1899–1971) (U.S. Supreme Court Justice) 53

Harpers Ferry 158

Helling v. McKinney 133, 140

Holmes, Oliver Wendell (U.S. Supreme Court Justice) 147

Housing Act of 1949 78, 81, 82

Housing and Community Development Act of 1974 78, 80

Hudson v. McMillan 139, 140

Hutton v. Finney 148

Individuals with Disabilities Education Act (IDEA) 69–70

"informal amendments" to the U.S. Constitution 78, 88, 136, 139, 142–143, 144, 148, 157

inherent power of courts 56

Jackson, Andrew 33, 34, 74, 155

Jefferson, Thomas 30, 31, 32, 33, 35, 37, 48, 75, 80, 125, 128, 133, 155

judicial power of the U.S. 45

Lacey Act of 1900 110

Leslie Salt Company v. United States 12, 105, 106

"liberty of contract" 17, 50

Lincoln, Abraham 33, 155

Lochner v. New York 50, 57

Louisiana ex rel. Francis v. Resweber 135, 143

Low Level Radioactive Waste Policy Amendments Act of 1985 99

Madison, James 28, 29, 30, 32, 34, 35, 44, 74
Marshall, John (Chief Justice of the U.S.) 31
Martin v. Hadix 144
Martin v. Hunter's Lessee 112, 129
Martin v. State of Kansas 89, 90
Meachum v. Fano 142, 149
"migratory bird rule"—commerce clause 107, 108
Minnesota v. Carter 47, 48
Mississippi Territory 60
Missouri Compromise 56
Morales v. Schmidt 142

National Association of Homebuilders v. Babbitt 114, 120
"National Code of Prison Regulation" 140
National Defense Education Act of 1958 65
National Endowment for the Arts v. Finley 127
National Foundation of the Arts Act of 1965 122
National Housing Act 77
National Labor Relations Act 38
National Labor Relations Board v. Jones & Laughlin Steel Corporation 37, 40
National Recovery Act of 1933 o.34, 35
Necessary and Proper Clause (U.S. Constitution) 32
"New Deal Amendment" 38, 39, 40, 41, 54, 78, 87, 95, 96, 99, 101, 102, 105, 106, 107, 108, 112, 114, 115, 116, 120
New York v. United States 97, 99, 104

"One Person—One Vote" 54
Osborn v. Bank of the United States 46

Pierce, Franklin 74
Plessy v. Ferguson 51
Pogo (cartoon character) 153
"police power" (states) 42
"pork barrel" legislation 80, 81, 83
Printz v. United States 100, 103
Prison Litigation Reform Act of 1995 149
Prohibition 39
Public Use (Amendment 5) 81–82, 83

"Reapportionment Amendment" 54
"Republicans" 29–30

Reynolds v. Sims 52, 53, 54
Rhodes v. Chapman 148
Robinson v. California 143
Roe v. Wade 16, 57, 158, 159
Roman Empire 19
Roosevelt, Franklin 34, 37, 41, 77, 119
Roosevelt, Theodore 156

San Antonio Independent School District v. Rodriguez 55, 66, 88
Sandin v. Conner 144
Schechter Poultry Corporation v. United States 34, 35, 36, 119
Schneider v. District of Columdia 82
segregation (racial) 51
"Separate but Equal" 51
separation of powers (Congress– Supreme Court) 91
slaves: right to own 17
Solid Waste Management Agency of Northern Cook County v. United States Army Corps of Engineers 108–109
South Dakota v. Dole 43, 44, 79
Spending Clause *see* Taxing for the general Welfare Clause
Stenberg v. Carhart 158
Steward Machine Co. v. Davis 74
Story, Joseph (U.S. Supreme Court Justice) 31, 35, 62, 118, 119
Strauder v. West Virginia 51
Stromberg v. California 147
"substantive due process" 55, 57

Taft, William Howard 152
Taxing for the General Welfare Clause (Spending Clause) 10, 36, 43, 44, 62, 65, 70, 73, 74, 79, 82, 101, 123
township (U.S. Government Survey) 60
Train v. Natural Resources Defense Council 95
treaty power 111, 112
Troxel v. Granville 18
TVA v. Hill 110

unfunded mandates 64
United States Code (Annotated): **16 USCA** *Sec. 667(e)* 110; *Sec. 701* 110; *Sec. 1531* 110; *Sec. 1532* 113; *Sec. 1538* 110, 111; **20 USCA** *Sec. 951* 122, 123, 128; *Sec. 954* 125; *Sec. 960* 125; *Sec. 1400* 69, 70, 71; *Sec. 1403* 72; *Sec. 1412* 70,71; *Sec. 1414* 71; *Sec. 1701* 67, 68; *Sec. 1702* 67; *Sec. 1703* 67; *Sec. 3402*

69; **23 USCA** *Sec. 131,* 154, 158 29; **33 USCA** *Sec. 1251* 102; *Sec. 1311* 103; *Sec. 1313* 103; *Sec. 1319* 103; *Sec. 1362(6)* 106; **42 USCA** *Sec. 1441* 78, 79, 82; *Sec. 5301* 78, 80; *Sec. 5303* 80; *Sec. 7410* 96, 97; *Sec. 7413* 97; *Sec. 12101* 84; *Sec. 12102* 84; *Sec. 12181* 85

United States Code of Federal Regulations: **33 CFR** *Sec. 323.2(c)* 105; *Sec. 328.3(a)* 105; **40 CFR** *Sec. 230.3(s)(3)* 105; **50 CFR** *Sec. 17.3* 113

United States Statutes at Large: *1 Stat. at 267* 60; *2 Stat. at 234* 60; *2 Stat. at 279* 61; *2 Stat. at 382–383* 61; *2 Stat. at 480* 61; *3 Stat. at 163* 61; *3 Stat. at 309* 61; *3 Stat. at 319* 61; *5 Stat. at 600* 61; *12 Stat. at 504* 61; *26 Stat. 417–418* 62; *31 Stat. 187* 110; *39 Stat. 929* 63, 64; *48 Stat. 1246* 77; *60 Stat. 790* 82; *62 Stat. 1155* 101; *63 Stat. 413* 77; *69 Stat. 322* 94; *79 Stat. 895* 122; *80 Stat. 925* 110; *83 Stat. 275* 110; *86 Stat. 816* 102; *86 Stat. at 844* 103; *86 Stat. at 846–847* 104; *87 Stat. 884* 110; *104 Stat. at 328–329* 84; *104 Stat. at 354* 85

United States v. Butler 119
United States v. Carlton 55
United States v. Darby 40, 86
United States v. District of Columbia 103
United States v. Duracell International, Inc. 103

United States v. Lopez 41, 88, 120
United States v. Morrison 43
United States v. Ohio Department of Highway Safety 95, 98, 99
United States v. Riverside Bayview Homes, Inc. 105, 106
United States v. Worrall 45
University of Alabama v. Garrett 90
urban redevelopment 82
U.S. Supreme Court: amending the Constitution 54, 83, 136, 139, 142–143, 144, 148; mistaken decisions 16, 17, 50, 51, 57

Vacco v. Quill 55
Van Buren, Martin 73
Voinovich v. Women's Professional Medical Corporation 158

Washington, George 28, 32, 33
Washington v. Glucksberg 17, 56, 57, 158, 159
Weems v. United States 135, 139
"Wetlands" commerce clause 105, 106, 107
Whitney v. California 147
"whole power of legislation"—States 10, 88
Wickard v. Filburn 40, 41, 86, 108
Wolff v. McDonnell 144